Leckie
the education publisher
for Scotland

Primary **Maths**
for Scotland

2nd Level Maths

2C

Practice Workbook 2

001/12092024

10 9 8 7 6 5 4 3 2 1

ISBN 9780008680381

Published by
Leckie
An imprint of HarperCollins Publishers
Westerhill Road, Bishopbriggs, Glasgow, G64 2QT

T: 0844 576 8126 F: 0844 576 8131
leckiescotland@harpercollins.co.uk www.leckiescotland.co.uk

HarperCollins Publishers
Macken House, 39/40 Mayor Street Upper, Dublin 1, D01 C9W8, Ireland

Publisher: Fiona McGlade

Special thanks
Project editor: Peter Dennis
Layout: Jouve
Proofreader: Julianna Dunn

A CIP Catalogue record for this book is available from the British Library.

Acknowledgements
Images © Shutterstock.com

Printed in the UK by Martins the Printers

Contents

Answers
Check your answers to this workbook online: https://collins.co.uk/pages/scottish-primary-maths

6.1 Converting fractions

1 Convert each of these improper fractions into a mixed number. The first one has been done for you.

$$\frac{5}{2} \qquad = \qquad 2\frac{1}{2}$$

a)

one half	one half	one half	one half	one half

two halves = one whole   two halves = one whole   one half

| one whole | one whole | | one half |

$$\frac{5}{2} = 2\frac{1}{2}$$

b)

one third	one third	one third	one third	one third

$$\frac{\Box}{\Box} = \Box\frac{\Box}{\Box}$$

c)

one quarter	one quarter	one quarter	one quarter	one quarter	one quarter	one quarter

$$\frac{\Box}{\Box} = \Box\frac{\Box}{\Box}$$

d)

one fifth	one fifth	one fifth	one fifth	one fifth	one fifth	one fifth	one fifth	one fifth	one fifth	one fifth

$$\frac{\Box}{\Box} = \Box\frac{\Box}{\Box}$$

2 Convert each of these mixed numbers into an improper fraction. The first one has been done for you.

$$2\frac{2}{3} \qquad = \qquad \frac{8}{3}$$

a)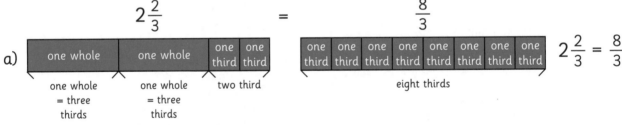

one whole = three thirds   one whole = three thirds   two third   eight thirds

$$2\frac{2}{3} = \frac{8}{3}$$

b)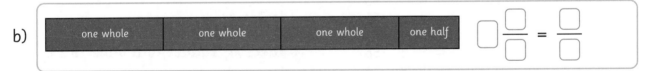

$$\Box\frac{\Box}{\Box} = \frac{\Box}{\Box}$$

c)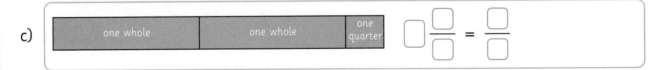

$$\Box\frac{\Box}{\Box} = \frac{\Box}{\Box}$$

d)

one whole	one fifth	one fifth	one fifth

$$\Box\frac{\Box}{\Box} = \frac{\Box}{\Box}$$

3 Write the improper fraction and the mixed number for each of these shaded diagrams. The first one has been done for you.

	Improper fraction	Mixed number
a)	$\dfrac{7}{4}$	$1\dfrac{3}{4}$
b)		
c)		
d)		

★ **Challenge**

a) Arrange these improper fractions in order, starting with the smallest:

$$\frac{31}{4} \qquad \frac{50}{7} \qquad \frac{15}{12}$$

b) Find two mixed numbers between:

$$4\frac{3}{14} \text{ and } 4\frac{2}{5}$$

1 Write a common equivalent to help you solve the following:

a) Nuria has completed three-quarters of a nature walk in a local park. Amman has completed four-fifths of the same walk. Who has walked further?

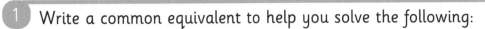

three-quarters   or   four-fifths

b) Finlay has filled three-quarters of a jar with sand. Isla has filled five-sixths of an identical jar with sand. Who has more sand in their jar?

three-quarters   or   five-sixths

2 Use equivalence to compare the following pairs of fractions. The first one has been done for you.

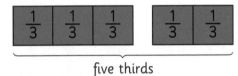

five thirds   three halves

a) $\dfrac{5}{3}$ and $\dfrac{3}{2}$

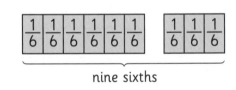

ten sixths   nine sixths

$\dfrac{10}{6}$ is greater than $\dfrac{9}{6}$ so $\dfrac{5}{3}$ is greater than $\dfrac{3}{2}$.

b) $\dfrac{5}{2}$ and $\dfrac{7}{4}$

c) $\dfrac{11}{5}$ and $\dfrac{5}{2}$

3 Write each of these improper fractions in the correct box on the number line:

$\frac{15}{4}$, $\frac{16}{5}$, $\frac{7}{2}$.

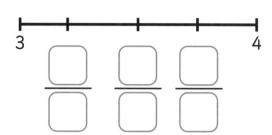

3   4

★ Challenge

22   5   3   16   7   19

a) Choose two of the orange cards to create an improper fraction that is less than 2.

b) Now choose two of the cards to create an improper fraction that is between 2 and 3.

c) Use two of the cards to create an improper fraction that is greater than 5.

6.3 Simplifying fractions

1 Use common factors to calculate an equivalent fraction in its simplest form for each of the following. Draw each fraction in its simplest form.

a)

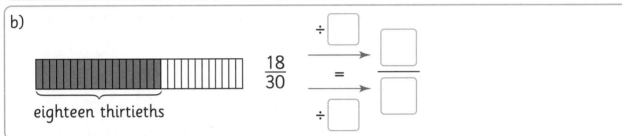

nine twelfths

$\dfrac{9}{12}$ $\overset{\div\ \boxed{}}{\underset{\div\ \boxed{}}{\Large=}}$ $\dfrac{\boxed{}}{\boxed{}}$

b)

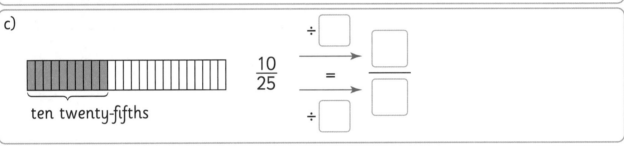

eighteen thirtieths

$\dfrac{18}{30}$ $\overset{\div\ \boxed{}}{\underset{\div\ \boxed{}}{\Large=}}$ $\dfrac{\boxed{}}{\boxed{}}$

c)

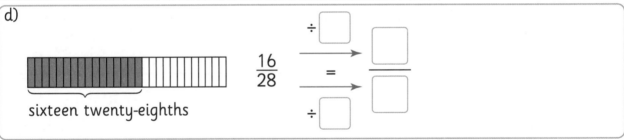

ten twenty-fifths

$\dfrac{10}{25}$ $\overset{\div\ \boxed{}}{\underset{\div\ \boxed{}}{\Large=}}$ $\dfrac{\boxed{}}{\boxed{}}$

d)

sixteen twenty-eighths

$\dfrac{16}{28}$ $\overset{\div\ \boxed{}}{\underset{\div\ \boxed{}}{\Large=}}$ $\dfrac{\boxed{}}{\boxed{}}$

2 Use common factors to calculate an equivalent fraction in its simplest form for each of these. The first one has been done for you. Remember to check to see if the fraction can be simplified further, like the first one.

a) $\dfrac{24}{40}$ $\overset{\div 4}{\underset{\div 4}{\Large=}}$ $\dfrac{6}{10}$ $\overset{\div 2}{\underset{\div 2}{\Large=}}$ $\dfrac{3}{5}$

b) $\dfrac{10}{40}$

c) $\dfrac{18}{27}$

d) $\dfrac{28}{36}$

e) $\dfrac{42}{60}$ [ ]

f) $\dfrac{32}{72}$ [ ]

3

a) Circle the fractions that would be $\dfrac{3}{5}$ in their simplest form:

$\dfrac{12}{20}$ $\dfrac{10}{15}$ $\dfrac{30}{50}$ $\dfrac{27}{45}$ $\dfrac{21}{30}$

b) Circle the fractions that give $\dfrac{4}{7}$ when they are written in their simplest form:

$\dfrac{80}{140}$ $\dfrac{32}{63}$ $\dfrac{20}{35}$ $\dfrac{24}{42}$ $\dfrac{8}{14}$

★ Challenge

Circle the fraction that is the odd one out here. Explain why you chose this one as the odd one out.

$\dfrac{50}{80}$ $\dfrac{45}{72}$ $\dfrac{10}{16}$ $\dfrac{30}{42}$ $\dfrac{25}{40}$

6.4 Adding and subtracting fractions

1 We can use equivalence to help when we are adding and subtracting fractions, like this:

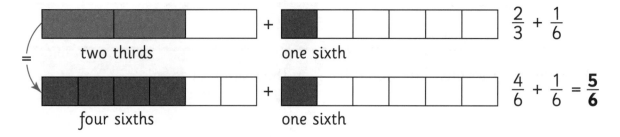

$\frac{2}{3} + \frac{1}{6}$

two thirds · one sixth

$\frac{4}{6} + \frac{1}{6} = \frac{5}{6}$

four sixths · one sixth

Use equivalence to solve the following:

a) one quarter · three eighths $\frac{1}{4} + \frac{3}{8} =$ ☐

b) one quarter · five eighths $\frac{1}{4} + \frac{5}{8} =$ ☐

c) two fifths · three tenths $\frac{2}{5} + \frac{3}{10} =$ ☐

d) four thirds · five sixths $\frac{4}{3} - \frac{5}{6} =$ ☐

2 Draw bar models to help solve the following:

a) $\frac{1}{2} + \frac{3}{8} =$ ☐

b) $\frac{11}{12} - \frac{2}{3} =$ ☐

c) $\frac{7}{10} + \frac{3}{5} =$ ☐

3 Draw diagrams to solve the following problems:

a) Amman and Isla went fishing. Amman caught a fish weighing $1\frac{2}{5}$ kg and Isla caught a fish weighing $1\frac{3}{10}$ kg. What is the total weight of the two fish?

b) A bottle contains $2\frac{5}{8}$ litres of water. Finlay pours $1\frac{1}{4}$ litres of the water into a jug. How much water is left in the bottle?

c) Nuria is cycling around a track that is $4\frac{5}{6}$ km long. So far, she has cycled $2\frac{2}{3}$ km. How far does she still have to cycle?

★ Challenge

Can you place the fractions in the correct place on the grid to make each calculation true? You may only use each fraction once.

$\frac{3}{5}$ $\frac{11}{12}$ $\frac{8}{9}$

$\frac{7}{10}$ $\frac{1}{10}$

$\frac{1}{4}$

$\frac{5}{6}$ $\frac{3}{8}$ $\frac{2}{9}$

a)		+		=	$\frac{7}{10}$
b)	$\frac{1}{8}$	+		=	
c)		−	$\frac{1}{5}$	=	$\frac{1}{2}$
d)		−		=	$\frac{1}{12}$
e)		+	$\frac{2}{3}$	=	

6.5 Converting decimal fractions to fractions

1 Draw lines to match the fraction shown by each bar to its decimal equivalent. One has been done for you.

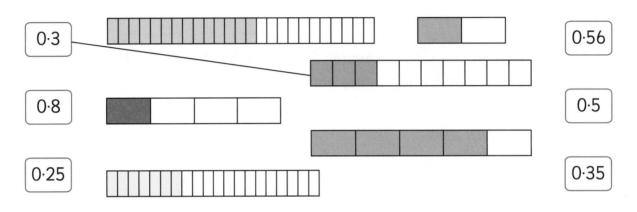

0.3   0.56

0.8   0.5

0.25   0.35

2 Write each of the following decimal fractions as a fraction, then as a fraction in its simplest form. The first one has been done for you.

Decimal fraction	Fraction	Simplified fraction
0·75	$\frac{75}{100}$	$\frac{3}{4}$
0·45		
0·62		
0·18		
0·56		

3 Match each of these decimal fractions to an equivalent fraction by drawing a lines between them.

Decimal fraction	0·65	0·7	0·75	0·66	0·6

Fraction	$\dfrac{3}{5}$	$\dfrac{7}{10}$	$\dfrac{33}{50}$	$\dfrac{14}{20}$	$\dfrac{3}{4}$	$\dfrac{13}{20}$

★ Challenge

a) Arrange these in order from smallest to largest.

$$0·79 \qquad \frac{4}{5} \qquad \frac{67}{100} \qquad 0·7 \qquad \frac{3}{4}$$

Write each number in the correct place on this line to give an ordered list from smallest to largest.

Smallest ⟶ Largest

☐ ☐ ☐ ☐ ☐

b) Write a fraction on this card to add in to the ordered list in part a. Your fraction must fit into the second place in the ordered list.

$$\boxed{\dfrac{}{}}$$

1 Draw a bar model to solve each of the following:

a) What is half of one-fifth of a bar?

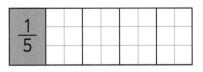

$$\frac{1}{2} \text{ of } \frac{1}{5} = \boxed{}$$

b) What is half of three-fifths of a bar?

$$\frac{1}{2} \text{ of } \frac{3}{5} = \boxed{}$$

c) What is one quarter of three-fifths of a bar?

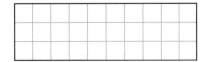

$$\frac{1}{4} \text{ of } \frac{3}{5} = \boxed{}$$

d) What is one third of three-quarters of a bar?

$$\frac{1}{3} \text{ of } \frac{3}{4} = \boxed{}$$

2 Draw a bar model to help you solve each of the following problems:

a) Amman has half a tub of paint. He uses one third of the paint during an art lesson. What fraction of a whole tub of paint did Amman use?

b) Isla and Nuria have one third of a bag of compost. They use three-quarters of the compost when planting some flowers. What fraction of a whole bag of compost did Isla and Nuria use?

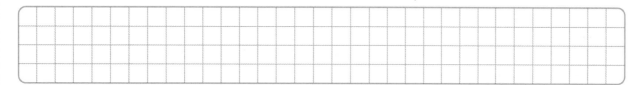

c) Finlay has two thirds of a roll of sticky tape. He uses one-quarter of the tape to wrap a parcel. What fraction of a whole roll of tape does Finlay use?

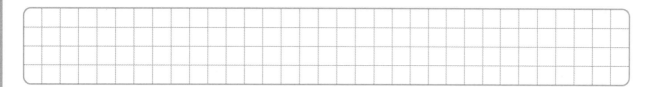

★ Challenge

Isla says: "I think $\frac{3}{4}$ of $\frac{2}{5}$ is the same as $\frac{2}{5}$ of $\frac{3}{4}$."

Nuria says: "No, that is not right. $\frac{3}{4}$ of $\frac{2}{5}$ is not the same as $\frac{2}{5}$ of $\frac{3}{4}$."

Do you agree with Isla or Nuria? Use bar models to help you explain your answer.

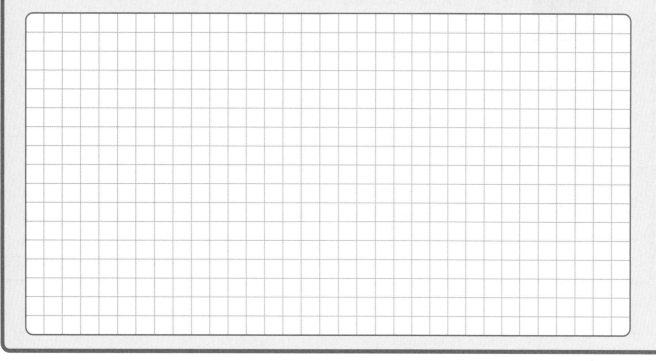

6.7 Dividing a fraction by a whole number

1 Use the blank bar models to work out how the following could be shared out equally. The first one has been done for you.

a) $\frac{1}{3}$ Shared between two people $\frac{1}{6}$ / $\frac{1}{6}$ $\frac{1}{3} \div 2 = \frac{1}{6}$ each

b) $\frac{1}{4}$ Shared between two people   _____

c) $\frac{1}{5}$ Shared between two people   _____

d) $\frac{1}{5}$ Shared between three people   _____

2 Use the blank bar models to work out how the following could be shared out equally.

a) $\frac{1}{4}$ $\frac{1}{4}$ $\frac{1}{4}$ Shared between two people   _____

b) $\frac{1}{3}$ $\frac{1}{3}$ Shared between two people   _____

c) $\frac{1}{5}$ $\frac{1}{5}$ $\frac{1}{5}$ Shared between three people   _____

d) $\frac{1}{6}$ $\frac{1}{6}$ $\frac{1}{6}$ $\frac{1}{6}$ $\frac{1}{6}$ Shared between four people   _____

3 Amman, Finlay and Nuria are sharing $\frac{5}{8}$ of a cake equally. What fraction of the cake do they each get?

★ Challenge

Work out the missing digits in these calculations.

a) $\dfrac{3}{\Box} \div 4 = \dfrac{3}{20}$

b) $\dfrac{\Box}{7} \div 2 = \dfrac{2}{7}$

c) $\dfrac{\Box}{\Box} \div 5 = \dfrac{3}{20}$

d) Make up two questions like these with missing digits to challenge a partner.
Your questions should involve dividing a proper fraction by a whole number.

6.8 Dividing a whole number by a fraction

1 The children are preparing fruit to make fruit pots for the school fair.

Calculate how many portions they can make from the following:

a) Five bananas to be divided into $\frac{1}{2}$ portions.

b) Seven apricots to be divided into $\frac{1}{2}$ portions.

c) Six mangos to be divided into $\frac{1}{2}$ portions.

d) Six pineapples to be divided into $\frac{1}{3}$ portions.

e) Four grapefruits to be divided into $\frac{1}{3}$ portions.

f) Eight pears to be divided into $\frac{1}{4}$ portions.

g) Nine melons to be divided into $\frac{1}{5}$ portions.

2

a) A chef makes 5 kilograms of pizza dough. If one pizza needs $\frac{1}{4}$ of a kilogram of pizza dough, how many pizzas can be made altogether from the 5 kilograms of dough?

b) The chef has 12 metres of foil to use for wrapping pizzas. If one pizza needs $\frac{3}{4}$ of a metre, how many pizzas can be wrapped from the 12 metres of foil?

⭐ **Challenge**

RIBBON

Blue:	Yellow:	Green:	White:
13 metres on each roll	10 metres on each roll	9 metres on each roll	11 metres on each roll

The children are ordering ribbon to use in a craft project. They do not mind what colour the ribbon is. They need to cut the ribbon into pieces that are $\frac{2}{3}$ metre long for their project.

a) How many pieces of ribbon $\frac{2}{3}$ metre long could be cut for each colour?

b) Which colour should they order if they do not want to waste any ribbon? Explain your answer.

1 Convert the following fractions into both a decimal and a percentage. The first one has been done for you.

a) $\dfrac{7}{10}$

$\dfrac{7}{10}$ = 0·7 = 70%

b) $\dfrac{3}{10}$

$\dfrac{3}{10}$ = [·] = [ ] %

c) $\dfrac{3}{5}$

$\dfrac{3}{5}$ = [·] = [ ] %

d) $\dfrac{1}{20}$

$\dfrac{1}{20}$ = [·] = [ ] %

e) $\dfrac{9}{20}$

$\dfrac{9}{20}$ = [·] = [ ] %

2 Convert each decimal fraction into a fraction in its simplest form, and a percentage. The first one has been done for you.

a) 0·25 = $\dfrac{25}{100}$ = $\dfrac{1}{4}$ = 25%

b) 0·75 = $\dfrac{\square}{\square}$ = $\dfrac{\square}{\square}$ = [ ] %

c) 0·32 = $\dfrac{\square}{\square}$ = $\dfrac{\square}{\square}$ = [ ] %

d) $\boxed{0.15}$ = $\dfrac{\boxed{}}{\boxed{}}$ = $\dfrac{\boxed{}}{\boxed{}}$ = $\boxed{}$ %

3) Amman and Finlay are converting 0·4 into a fraction in its simplest form.

Amman says: I think it is $\dfrac{2}{5}$ and Finlay says: No, it is $\dfrac{1}{25}$.

Who do you agree with? Explain your answer.

★ Challenge

Isla has made up clues for an unknown fraction:

- The numerator and the denominator each have exactly two digits.
- The numerator has a 1 in it.
- The denominator has a 4 in it.
- When expressed as a percentage it is less than 45%.

Can you find 4 different possibilities for Isla's fraction, each with a different denominator?

$\dfrac{\boxed{}}{\boxed{}}$ $\dfrac{\boxed{}}{\boxed{}}$ $\dfrac{\boxed{}}{\boxed{}}$ $\dfrac{\boxed{}}{\boxed{}}$

1 Use the bar models to work out the following:

1650

a) $\frac{3}{5}$ of 1650

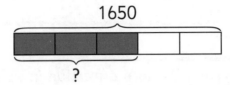

?

b) 60% of 4500

4500

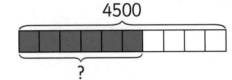

?

2 Make up a word problem for each of these bar models then solve the problem:

620

a)

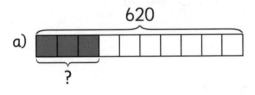

?

96

b)

?

3 A school is aiming to collect a total of £2400 to pay for a sports trip to France. 30% of this total has been raised so far. How much money still needs to be collected to reach the total?

★ Challenge

The children are testing their fitness in the school health suite. They each noted their results in this table but some of the totals got smudged. Can you work out what each child's total was and convert this to a percentage?

	TEST 1	TEST 2	TEST 1 + TEST 2 TOTAL	FINAL %
FITNESS TEST RESULTS				
Amman	$\dfrac{14}{20}$	60%	$\dfrac{130}{200}$	65%
Finlay	$\dfrac{4}{5}$	$\dfrac{39}{50}$	$\dfrac{}{200}$	
Isla	64%	$\dfrac{7}{10}$	$\dfrac{}{200}$	
Nuria	42%	$\dfrac{11}{25}$	$\dfrac{}{200}$	

7.1 Money problems using the four operations

1 Amman needs to order ink for his printer. He sees these three options on the internet.

Pronto Print
£45·20
FREE DELIVERY

Speedy Ink
£43
DELIVERY £1·80

Computer Supplies
£42
DELIVERY £3·50

a) What is the lowest price Amman could pay and which company is this from? Use your working to explain your thinking.

b) Amman wants to buy 6 packs of printer paper.

Pronto Print
Printer paper: 1 pack £4·95
5 packs £22·75

Computer Supplies
Printer paper special offer:
3 packs £13·50

Which company will he get the best deal from? Use your working to explain your thinking.

2 Isla is planning activities for a school holiday. She says:

> I will go swimming on Monday and Tuesday. On Wednesday I will go for a swim then go to the gym.

One swim	£3·60
One swim + gym session	£5·80
Special ticket: three swims + two gym sessions	£14

Should Isla buy a Special ticket? Explain your answer.

★ Challenge

The children did some baking for a cake stall at a coffee morning. They baked 40 cupcakes to sell at £1·50 each and 35 flapjacks to sell at £1·20 each. They also made 60 chocolate brownies.

a) The children would like to raise at least £200 from the sale of their baking. How much do you think they should charge for a chocolate brownie?

b) Amman brings along a cheesecake that can be cut into 12 large slices or 20 small slices. Amman aims to raise at least £20 from the sale of his cheesecake.

How do you think he should cut the cheesecake up and what should he charge for each slice?

1 Look at the following budget plan for a dance club over a 4-week period and answer the questions.

		CREDIT	DEBIT
Income	(£320 per week)	£1280	
Hall rent	(£75 per week)		£300
Teacher's fee	(£80 per week)		£320
Electricity	(£45 per week)		£180
Heating	(£40 per week)		£160
TOTALS		**£1280**	**£960**

a) How much does the dance club have left after all the bills have been paid for this 4-week period?

b) If the dance club decides to get a mobile phone that costs £4·50 a week, how much will they have left at the end of the 4-week period?

2 Mr and Mrs Willis earn £1650 a month from their gardening business. Their mortgage is £800 a month and they spend £65 a week on food. How much do they have left over to spend on other things each month?

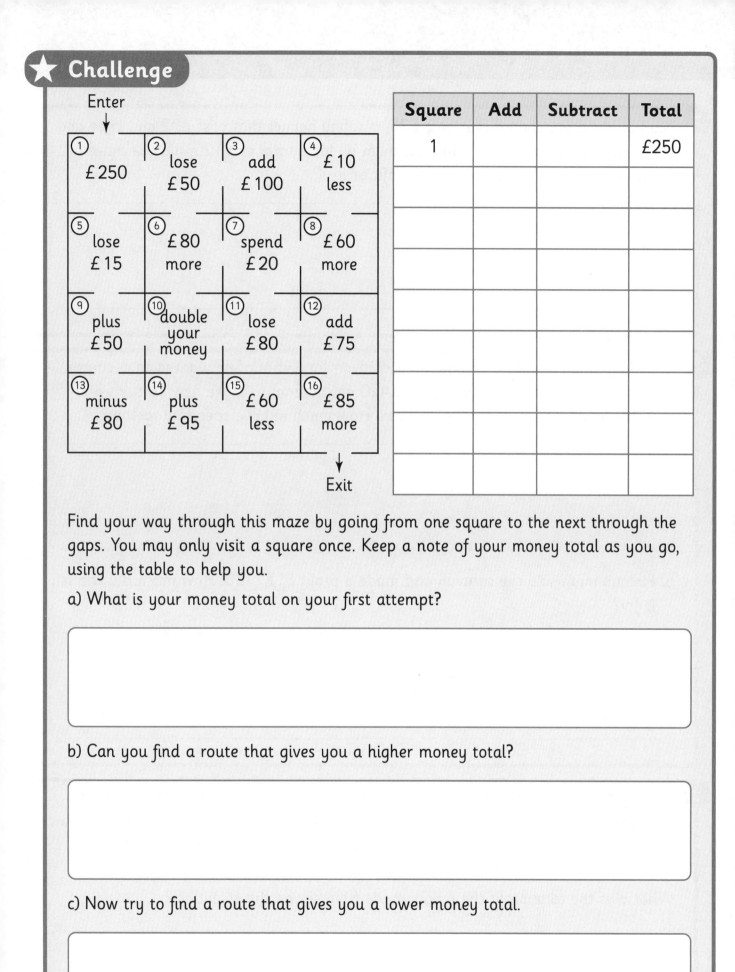

Enter ↓

1 ① £250	2 ② lose £50	3 ③ add £100	4 ④ £10 less
5 ⑤ lose £15	6 ⑥ £80 more	7 ⑦ spend £20	8 ⑧ £60 more
9 ⑨ plus £50	10 ⑩ double your money	11 ⑪ lose £80	12 ⑫ add £75
13 ⑬ minus £80	14 ⑭ plus £95	15 ⑮ £60 less	16 ⑯ £85 more

Exit ↓

Square	Add	Subtract	Total
1			£250

Find your way through this maze by going from one square to the next through the gaps. You may only visit a square once. Keep a note of your money total as you go, using the table to help you.

a) What is your money total on your first attempt?

b) Can you find a route that gives you a higher money total?

c) Now try to find a route that gives you a lower money total.

7.3 Profit and loss

1 Isla bought a skateboard that cost £75, a safety helmet that cost £32 and knee and elbow pads that cost £26. If she sold them all for a total of £120, did she make a profit or a loss? How much was the profit or loss?

2 a) Finlay's mum bought a second-hand caravan for £4560. She wanted to decorate the caravan, then sell it. She spent £420 on material to make new curtains and £390 on new flooring for the caravan. How much did she spend altogether?

b) Finlay's mum sold the caravan and made a profit of £1130. How much did she sell it for?

3 The children's school made 180 calendars to sell at a Christmas fair. The total cost of making the calendars was £215. At the fair, they sold 120 calendars for £4 each before Christmas. After Christmas, the remaining 60 calendars were sold at a reduced price of £1·50 each.

What was the total profit the school made from selling the calendars?

The Parent Council organised a raffle to raise funds for school playground equipment. There were three prizes:

1st prize: £90 voucher

2nd prize: £50 voucher

3rd prize: £30 voucher

The printing of tickets and posters for the raffle cost £40.

The Parent Council plan on selling 140 tickets.

a) Calculate how much each ticket would cost if, after the vouchers had been purchased and the printing paid for, there was no profit. This is called the 'break-even' price.

b) After the vouchers had been purchased and the printing had been paid for, Finlay noticed that the profit for the raffle was exactly the same as the costs of the prizes and printing. What would be the cost of each ticket to create this profit?

c) If 170 tickets are sold, the prizes remain the same and the cost of printing is still £40, how much would each ticket need to cost to make a profit of £385?

1 Nuria wants to buy a new tennis racquet that costs £55.

A sports shop has a sale giving 20% off all tennis equipment. What is the price of the tennis racquet after 20% has been deducted?

20% off

2

Buy one, get one half-price

COMFY CLOTHING
AMAZING OFFERS

20% off all clothing

Amman wants to buy two new hoodies. He sees some that cost £18 each in a shop with an offer of "buy one get one half-price". The store is also offering 20% off all clothing. Amman can only choose one of the offers.

a) Which offer will save Amman the most money?

b) How much does Amman save on the full price of two hoodies?

3 This leaflet shows the ticket prices for entry to a museum.

Adult ticket	£15
Child ticket	£10
Family ticket A (2 adults, 2 children)	£46·50
Family ticket B (1 adult, 3 children)	£44

The Kaur family need to buy tickets for 2 adults and 4 children.

Work out the cheapest way for them to do this.

★ Challenge

The children's teacher is planning a class outing to either the cinema or the theatre. Ticket prices and discount offers for each are shown here.

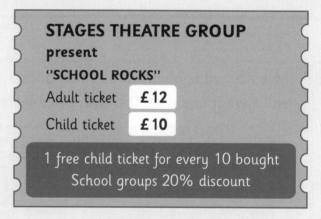

ORION CINEMA

Adult ticket £10

Child ticket £7

Loyalty card holders 10% discount

STAGES THEATRE GROUP
present
''SCHOOL ROCKS''
Adult ticket £12
Child ticket £10

1 free child ticket for every 10 bought
School groups 20% discount

The teacher has a loyalty card for the cinema.

30 children and 5 adults will be going on the outing. Will it be cheaper to buy tickets for the cinema or the theatre? Use your working to explain your thinking.

Cinema	Theatre

1 Mr Higgins wants to buy an electric bike that costs £650.

CYCLE SHACK

Electric bike	**£650**
Finance availabe:	
Deposit	£100
12 monthly payments of	£55

If Mr Higgins buys the bike using the finance available, how much will he pay altogether?

2 Mrs Ahmed is going to buy this games console. She wants to know how much she will save if she pays the cash price instead of paying in instalments.

GAMING DIRECT

Games console cash price.................................£475

Or pay in instalments:
Deposit..£90

6 monthly payments of..................................£70

How much money will Mrs Ahmed save if she pays the cash price?

3

SOFA CENTRAL

Hire purchase available at no extra cost.

No deposit required.

Annabel sees this special offer of hire purchase at no extra charge and decides to buy a sofa that costs £1195. She chooses to make six equal monthly payments of £175. How much will Annabel have to pay in the seventh month to pay the sofa off?

★ **Challenge**

Hire purchase is available on a family holiday to EuroWorld.

EUROWORLD

Family holiday for 2 adults + 2 children

Deposit **£800 + 18 monthly payments** of **£240**

Special Offer
20% off the hire-purchase price for full payment when booking.

The McKay family decide to take advantage of the special offer and pay for the holiday when they book.

a) How much do they pay for their holiday? Show all of your working.

b) What do the McKay family save by paying for their holiday when they book?

8.1 Investigating how long a journey will take

1 Amman and his family are travelling from Glasgow to Inverness by train. The journey takes 3 hours and 10 minutes. If they leave Glasgow at 11·50 am, what time will they arrive in Inverness?

2 A school trip to London is being planned. The organisers need to decide if they will travel by bus, train or aeroplane.

- Going by bus takes 12 hours and 20 minutes
- Going by train takes 6 hours and 45 minutes
- Going by aeroplane takes 1 hour 25 minutes

a) If they decide to go by bus and leave at 6 am, what time will they arrive in London?

b) A flight arrives in London at 3·55 pm. What time does it leave?

c) If they want to arrive in London by 3 pm and decide to go by train, what is the latest time they can catch a train?

3 Two trains travel on the same route between Montrose and Glasgow:

First train: leaves Montrose at 8·40 am and arrives in Glasgow at 10·58 am

Second train: leaves Montrose at 1·12 pm and arrives in Glasgow at 3·04 pm

Which train do you think makes the most stops? Explain your thinking.

★ Challenge

The children took part in an outdoor activities event. Isla and Nuria were in one group and Amman and Finlay were in a different group.

This is Isla's report of their activities:

We left the outdoor centre at 10 am. We started with a 10 minute walk to the loch. Then we got in and swam to the other side. This took us 25 minutes. When we got out we had 15 minutes to get dried and changed before we got on bikes and cycled for 45 minutes to the barbecue area.

Amman wrote this to say what his group did:

We got off the bus at 9·45 am. 15 minutes later we got into kayaks. We paddled across the loch for 50 minutes. We took 10 minutes to get out of the kayaks and get ready for our run. We ran for 20 minutes before we realised we were lost. We spent 5 minutes getting back to the track then we ran for 15 minutes. We were glad to arrive at the barbecue area.

Which group arrived at the barbecue area first? Show your working.

1 The children are at an outdoor activities park. They see this list of activities that they can take part in.

Nature walk	starts at 10·15 am	lasts 1 hour 20 minutes
Kayaking	starts at 10·30 am	lasts 2 hours 30 minutes
Mountain bike tour	starts at 10·40 am	lasts 3 hours 15 minutes

a) The start of the nature walk is delayed by 10 minutes. What time will it finish now?

b) Finlay and Nuria need to catch the bus home at 1·45 pm. Can they go on the mountain bike tour? Explain your answer.

2 As a birthday treat, Nuria is going on the Seabirds and Seals Cruise.

Nuria is on the boat for 15 minutes before it leaves and 10 minutes after it returns. How long is she on the boat for altogether?

RIVER FORTH BOAT TRIPS

Seabirds and Seals Cruise

Leaving at 11·35 am
Returning at 2·10 pm

Challenge

The children are planning a trip to the cinema to see a movie called Marvellous Monsters that begins at 2 pm. They will meet in the town centre and take a bus on route 32 to the cinema.

 **ORION CINEMA**

Special screening of MARVELLOUS MONSTERS At 2 pm

BUS ROUTE 32					
Town centre	11·15 am	11·50 am	12·20 pm	1·00 pm	1·20 pm
Swimming pool	11·18 am	–	12·23 pm	–	1·23 pm
Retail park	–	11·55 am	12·25 pm	–	1·25 pm
High school	11·25 am	–	12·30 pm	–	1·30 pm
Park and ride	11·30 am	12·05 pm	12·35 pm	1·12 pm	1·35 pm
Cinema	11·33 am	12·08 pm	12·35 pm	1·15 pm	1·38 pm

Isla says:

When we get off the bus it will take us 12 minutes to walk to the cinema.

Amman says:

We need to have 10 minutes to pick up our cinema tickets.

Nuria says:

I want to go to the kiosk when I get there to get a drink and a snack.

Finlay says:

Yes! Let's all go to the kiosk together before we go into the movie.

Which bus do you think the children should catch for their cinema trip? Explain your thinking.

8.3 Investigating ways speed, time and distance can be measured

1 Use the formula **time = distance ÷ speed** to calculate the time taken for each of these journeys:

a) Nuria walked 12 miles at 3 mph.

hours

b) An athlete ran 15 km at 5 kph.

hours

c) A bus travelled 350 miles at 50 mph.

hours

d) Amman cycled 28 km at 7 kph.

hours

2 Use the formula **speed = distance ÷ time** to calculate the average speed of these journeys:

a) A lorry travelled 120 miles in 3 hours.

b) A car was driven 120 miles in 2 hours.

c) A helicopter flew 480 km in 4 hours.

d) A swimmer swam 1500 metres in 50 minutes.

3 Use the formula **distance = speed × time** to calculate how far each of the following travelled:

a) A bike was ridden at a speed of 20 kph for 2 hours.

b) A car was driven at a speed of 60 mph for 3 hours.

c) A bird flew for 5 hours at a speed of 25 mph.

d) A train travelled for 4 hours at a speed of 125 kph.

4 Choose the correct formula to work out each of these.

a) A motorcycle was driven at 45 kph for 2 hours. How far was the journey?

b) A drone flew 180 metres at a speed of 9 metres per second. How long did the drone's journey take?

★ **Challenge**

A car travelled for 90 minutes at a speed of 50 mph. How far did the car travel?

1 The children are taking part in a construction challenge. They time each other building a tower using 25 modelling bricks

Here are the children's times, shown on a stopwatch.

Amman's time: 03:21 32

Finlay's time: 02:50 85

Isla's time: 03:09 02

Nuria's time: 02:58 10

a) Who took the longest time to build their tower?

b) Who completed the task in the shortest time?

c) Write the children's names in order of finishing the task, from quickest to slowest.

2 Three runners in a 2 km fun run wrote down their **target** finish times before they started running:

Eleanor	15 minutes and 30 seconds
Aisha	12 minutes
Neda	13 minutes

These stopwatches show the **actual** time each runner took in the fun run:

Eleanor's time: 13:15 07

Alisha's time: 13:28 68

Neda's time: 12:55 00

a) Who took less time to run the 2 km than their target time?

b) Who in this group of three runners was first to cross the finishing line?

c) Neda was very happy to beat her target time. How much did she beat her target time by?

★ Challenge

Fill in the blanks to complete the table. The first one has been done for you.

START TIME	FINISH TIME	TIME ELAPSED
04:07 16	08:19 23	4 minutes, 12 seconds, 7 centiseconds
12:15 28	15:23 32	
06:31 15		8 minutes, 15 seconds, 21 centiseconds
	24:08 49	3 minutes, 5 seconds, 18 centiseconds
		12 minutes, 50 seconds, 3 centiseconds

8.5 Converting between units of time

1 Convert the following from seconds to minutes:

a) 180 seconds

b) 360 seconds

c) 720 seconds

d) 1500 seconds

2 Convert the following from minutes to hours and minutes:

a) 120 minutes

120 minutes = _____ hours _____ minutes

b) 150 minutes

150 minutes = _____ hours _____ minutes

c) 270 minutes

270 minutes = _____ hours _____ minutes

d) 690 minutes

690 minutes = _____ hours _____ minutes

3 Convert the following from hours to days:

a) 48 hours

b) 120 hours

c) 216 hours

d) 600 hours

★ Challenge

a) Sort these times into ascending order, starting with the shortest time:

0·5 hours   72 minutes   6,000 seconds   95 minutes   2·75 hours   3,240 seconds

b) Sort these times into descending order, starting with the longest time:

3 years   116 weeks   42 months   260 weeks   2·5 years   35 months

1 A laser measuring device was used to find measurements in the school outdoor area.

The device gave the measurements in metres, but they need to be converted into centimetres.

Convert each of these lengths into centimetres and write your answers in the blank boxes above the measurements. The first one has been done for you.

SCHOOL OUTDOOR AREA

Trim trail

[   ] by [   ]

4·65 m   by   2·15 m

Greenhouse

[   ] by [   ]

2·4 m by   2 m

Vegetable garden

[   ] by [   ]

3·59 m   by   3·10 m

Recycling bins

[   ] by [   ]

3·2 m by 2·5 m

Bike racks

[   ] by [   ]

2·1 m by 3·04 m

Play equipment

[   ] by [   ]

6·79 m   by   5·28 m

Covered shelter

[   ] by [   ]

4·92 m   by   3·11 m

2 The children were finding out about bridges. They wrote down the lengths in metres of these two bridges in Scotland. Convert each of these lengths into kilometres.

a) Forth Road Bridge: 2512 metres

b) Queensferry Crossing: 2700 metres

3 The following list gives the diameter in millimetres of coins with a value of less than £1.

Convert each of these lengths into centimetres.

Coin	Diameter in mm	Diameter in cm
1p	20·3 mm	
2p	25·9 mm	
5p	18·0 mm	
10p	24·5 mm	
20p	21·4 mm	
50p	27·3 mm	

A sunflower was measured three times a week for five weeks. This table shows how much it had grown each time it was measured.

	Monday	Wednesday	Friday
Week 1	8·4 cm	75 mm	9·8 cm
Week 2	109 mm	10·2 cm	4 cm
Week 3	18·4 cm	42 mm	8·7 cm
Week 4	2·6 cm	12·5 cm	0·34 m
Week 5	45 mm	16 mm	26 mm

a) At the beginning of week 1, the sunflower measured 3·1 cm. Complete this table to show the height of the sunflower after each measurement. The first week has been filled in for you.

	Monday	Wednesday	Friday
Week 1	3·1 cm + 8·4 cm = 11·5 cm	11·5 cm + 75 mm = 19 cm	19 cm + 9·8 cm = 28·8 cm
Week 2			
Week 3			
Week 4			
Week 5			

b) The gardener thinks it grew most in Week 5. Do you agree? Explain your thinking.

Why don't you try to grow sunflowers and measure their height once they start growing?

9.2 Estimating and measuring mass

1 Amman and Isla are making a traybake to serve at a school open day. They are weighing the ingredients using digital scales that show mass in kilograms.

Write the mass of each ingredient in grams.

a) Butter

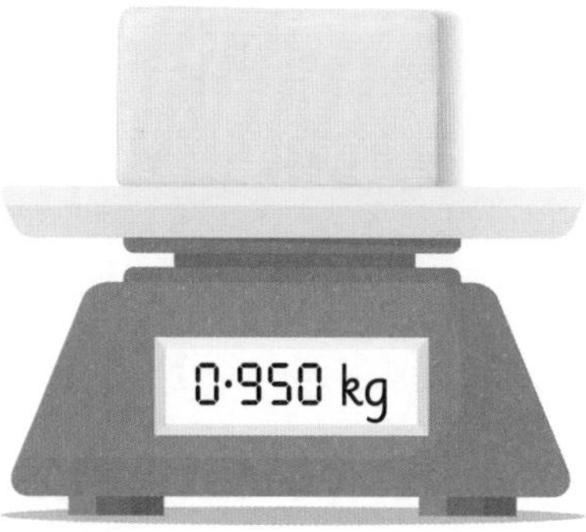

0·950 kg

b) Golden syrup

0·625 kg

c) Brown sugar

0·710 kg

d) Oats

1·385 kg

e) Dried fruit

1·115 kg

f) Milk chocolate

0·345 kg

2 Write these in ascending order, starting with the lightest:

2385 g   1·95 kg   2·55 kg   985 g   0·649 kg

3 Mrs Pearson checks the mass of her hand luggage before she leaves for the airport.

She knows that she must not take more than 7·5 kg with her onto the flight.

Mrs Pearson's scales are difficult to read, but she estimates that they are showing around 6 kg for the mass of her hand luggage.

MEAL DEAL

Sandwich   280 g
500 ml water   500 g
Potato crisps   40 g

At the airport, Mrs Pearson buys a meal deal to take onto the aeroplane with her. She also buys a hardback book that has a mass of 850 g. She puts the meal deal and the book into her hand luggage.

Do you think Mrs Pearson will be allowed to board the aeroplane?

Explain your answer.

At an autumn fair there is a pumpkin growing competition.

Points are given according to the mass of the pumpkin, with 1 point being awarded for every gram. Here are the results of the competition:

PUMPKIN GROWING COMPETITION

First place	4050 points
Second place	4007 points
Third place	3960 points

a) Write down the mass of each prize-winning pumpkin in kilograms.

b) One of the entrants goes to the judge to complain, saying:

> I should have 3rd prize because my pumpkin weighs 3 kilograms and 98 grams.

How do you think the judge will explain the results to this person?

1 Calculate the area of these rectangles. The first one has been partitioned for you.

a)

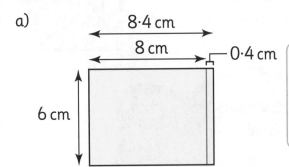

b)

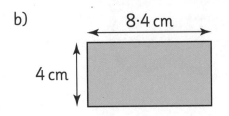

c)

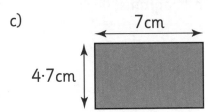

2 Find the missing length for each of these windows:

a)

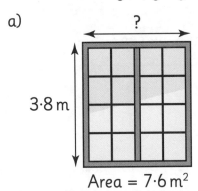

Area = 7·6 m²

b)

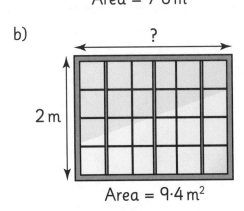

Area = 9·4 m²

3 Simon is choosing a rug for his room, which has an area of 6 m². He wants the rug to cover as much of the floor as possible. Tick the rug he should choose. Show your working.

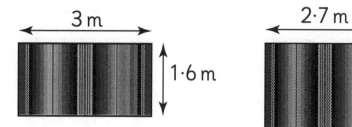

3 m   1·6 m   2·7 m   2 m

★ **Challenge**

Finlay and Nuria have each been asked to draw a rectangle with an area of 10·26 cm².

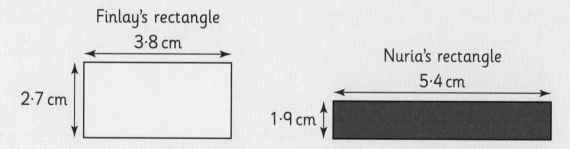

Finlay's rectangle
3·8 cm
2·7 cm

Nuria's rectangle
5·4 cm
1·9 cm

Have they done this correctly? Explain your thinking.

9.4 Estimating and measuring capacity

1

a) The children have poured water into jugs for a science experiment.
Write how much water each jug contains in both millilitres and litres.

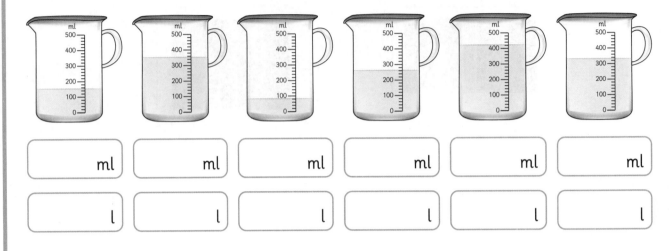

ml	ml	ml	ml	ml	ml
l	l	l	l	l	l

b) The experiment needs the children to pour exactly 1 litre of water into a bowl.
Can they do this using the amounts they have? Explain your answer.

2 Draw a line on the jug to show the given volume of liquid. Shade in the liquid below the line.

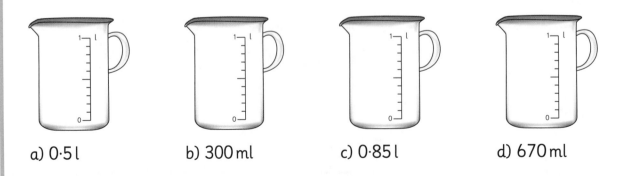

a) 0·5 l   b) 300 ml   c) 0·85 l   d) 670 ml

3 A bottle contains 2 litres of milk. Two glasses of milk are poured from the bottle, one containing 200 ml and the other containing 350 ml.

200 ml

350 ml

ml

l

How much milk will be left in the bottle? Give your answer in millilitres and also in litres.

★ **Challenge**

You have 1·5 litres of orange squash to share equally between three containers: a carton, a bottle and a jug.

Jug

Bottle

Carton

Each container holds at least 300 ml of liquid. The carton holds more than the bottle but less than the jug.

Using this information, can you find two different ways of sharing the orange squash?

9.5 Estimating imperial measurements

1 The average length of a jaguar from nose to tail is 9 feet. Compare this to the other big cats shown here and use it to estimate the average length of each one in feet.

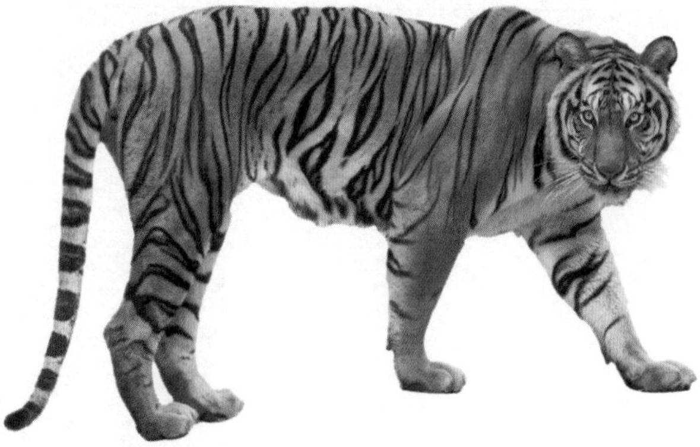

Tiger [ ]

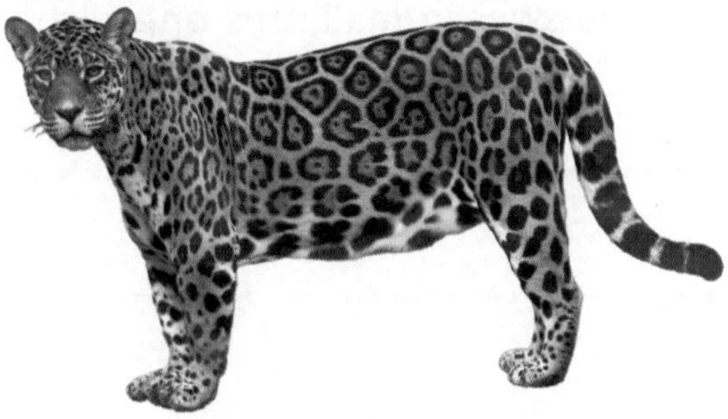

Jaguar [9 feet]

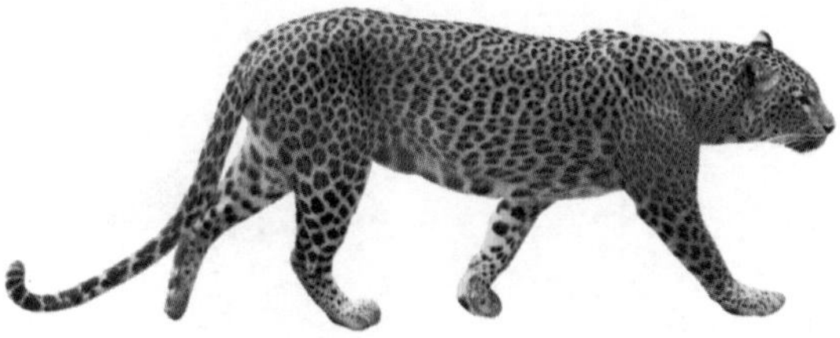

Leopard [ ]

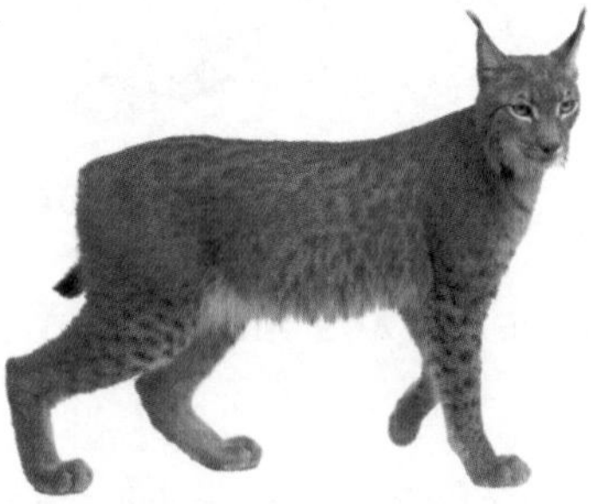

Lynx [ ]

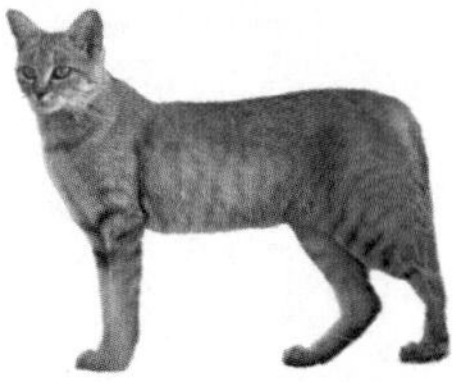

Wildcat [ ]

2 This map shows some of the main UK airports. The distance between Edinburgh airport and Inverness airport is 150 miles. Estimate the distance for each of the following:

a) Manchester airport and Glasgow airport

b) London Heathrow airport and Aberdeen airport

c) Newcastle airport and Bristol airport

d) Inverness airport and London Heathrow airport

e) Aberdeen airport and Inverness airport

f) Manchester airport and Inverness airport

SHETLAND ISLES

INVERNESS
ABERDEEN
EDINBURGH
GLASGOW
NEWCASTLE
MANCHESTER
BRISTOL
LONDON HEATHROW

★ Challenge

1 pound = 0·45 kilograms

1 kilogram = 2·2 pounds

4 oranges **or** 4 bananas have a mass of roughly one pound.

Use this to help you to work out the mass of 6 oranges **and** 4 bananas in kilograms.

9.6 Converting imperial measurements

Use the following to convert between metric and imperial measurements:

Length	Mass	Capacity
1 inch = 2·54 cm	1 ounce = 28·3 g	1 fluid ounce = 28·4 ml
1 foot = 30·5 cm	1 kg = 2·2 pounds	1 cup = 240 ml
1 yard = 91·4 cm	1 stone = 6·35 kg	1 litre = 1·76 pints
1 mile = 1·61 km		1 gallon = 4·55 litres

1 Convert the following:

a) 18 inches to cm

b) 78 kg to stones

c) 15 fluid ounces to ml

d) 12 pints to litres

2 The measurements for a tennis court are given here in feet.

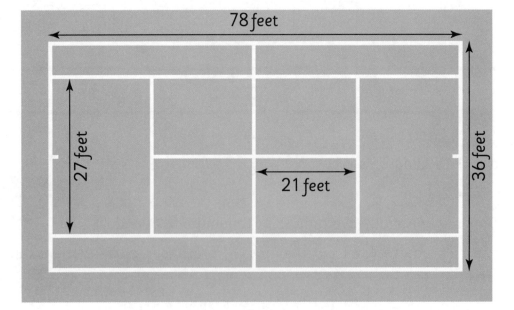

78 feet

27 feet

21 feet

36 feet

Convert each of the measurements to both metres and centimetres.

a) 78 feet

☐ ☐

b) 36 feet

☐ ☐

c) 27 feet

☐ ☐

d) 21 feet

☐ ☐

★ Challenge

Arrange each of these into ascending order, starting with the smallest:

a) 80 feet; 3000 inches; ½ kilometre; 15 yards; 120 metres

☐

b) 2 pounds; ¼ kilogram; ½ stone; 16 ounces; 702 grams

☐

c) 50 fluid ounces; 13 cups; 2 litres; 1 gallon; ½ pint

☐

1 Calculate the perimeter of each of the shapes below:

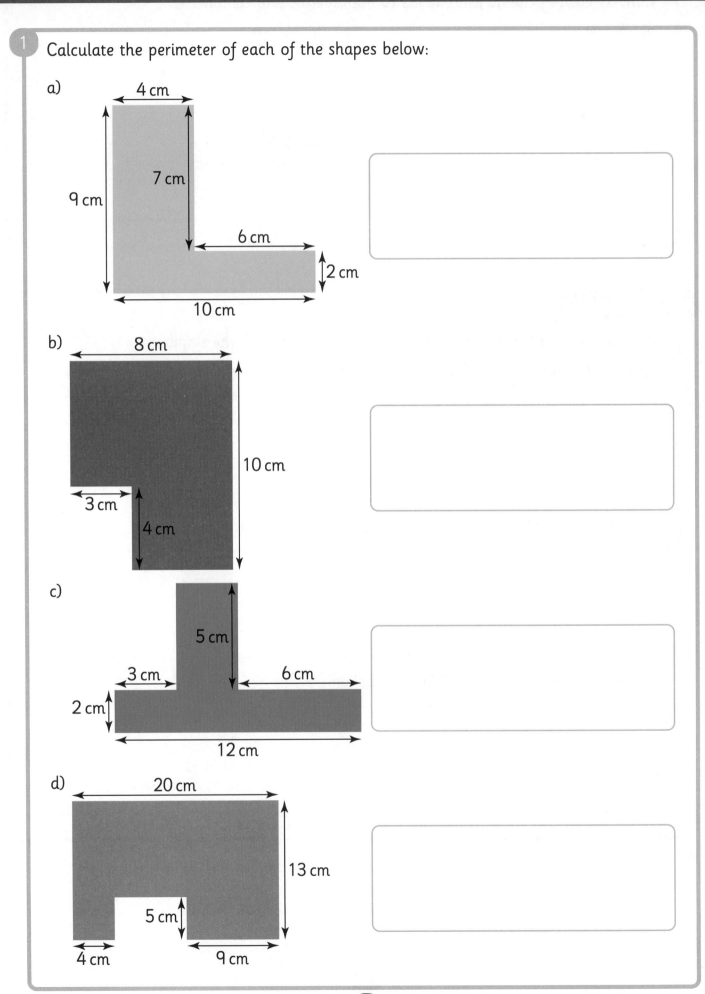

a)

4 cm

7 cm

9 cm

6 cm

2 cm

10 cm

b)

8 cm

10 cm

3 cm

4 cm

c)

5 cm

3 cm

6 cm

2 cm

12 cm

d)

20 cm

13 cm

5 cm

4 cm

9 cm

2 This is a plan of a community garden.

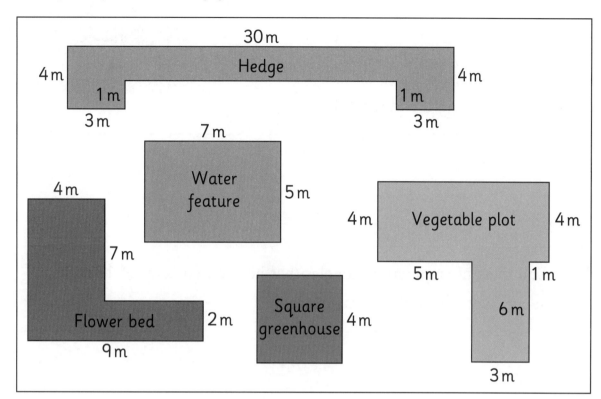

Calculate the perimeter of each area in the garden.

a) Hedge

b) Water feature

c) Greenhouse

d) Flower bed

e) Vegetable plot

3 A rectangle has a perimeter of 18 cm.

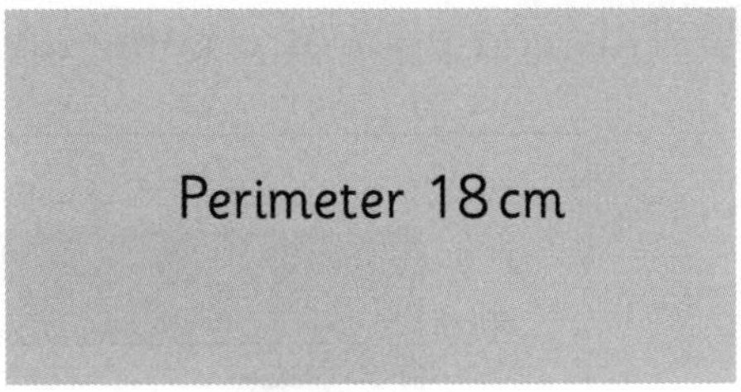

Perimeter 18 cm

a) What could its length and width be?

b) Can you think of any more rectangles that have a perimeter of 18 cm?
   If you can, write down their dimensions.

★ Challenge

The top of a desk is in the shape of a rectangle. The length of the desk is 45 cm more than its width. If the perimeter of the desk is 6·3 m, calculate its length and width.

1 Calculate the area of each of the following:

a)

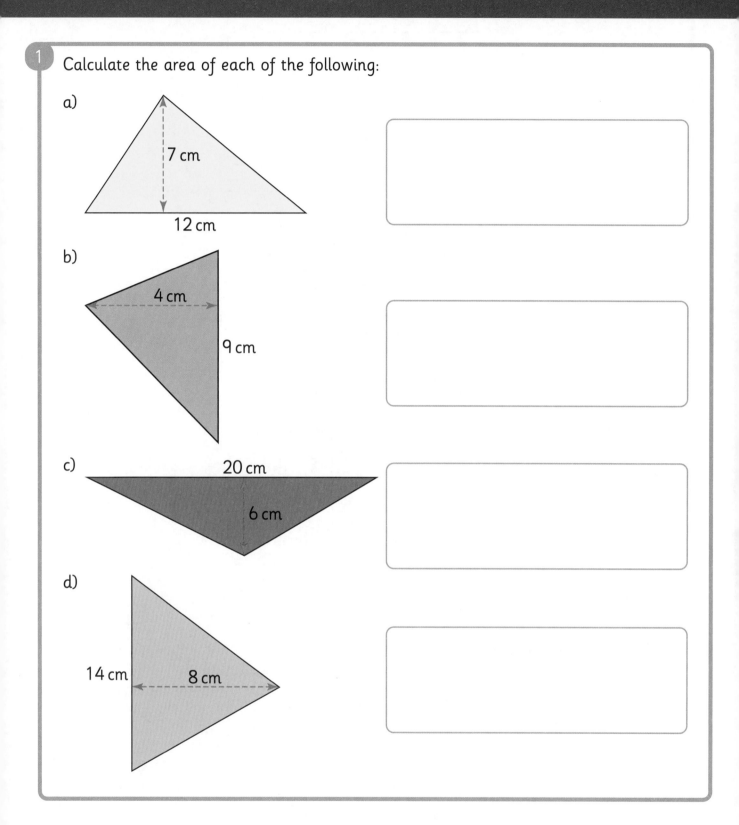

7 cm

12 cm

b)

4 cm

9 cm

c)

20 cm

6 cm

d)

14 cm   8 cm

2

a) Draw a triangle that has an area of 15 cm².

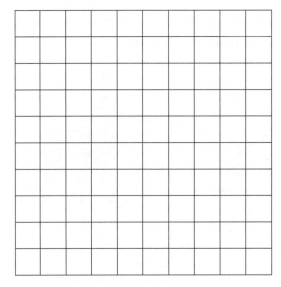

b) Draw a triangle that has an area of 18 cm².

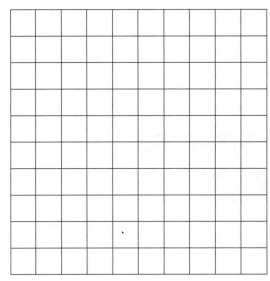

c) Draw a triangle that has an area of 24 cm².

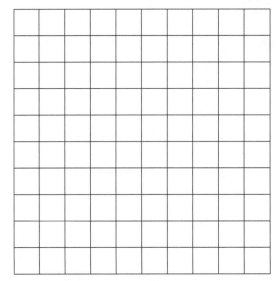

3 These two triangles have the same area. Calculate the missing length, shown by **?** on the diagram.

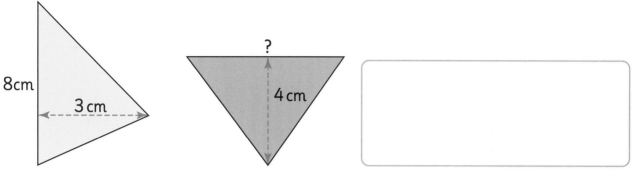

⭐ **Challenge**

The area of a triangle is greater than 13 cm² but less than 15 cm². The triangle's length is three times greater than its height. Can you work out what the length and height of this triangle might be?

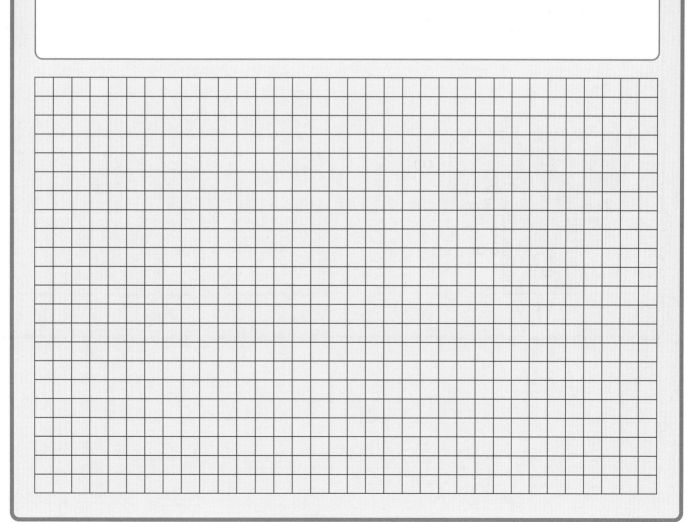

1 Calculate the area of each of these shapes:

a)

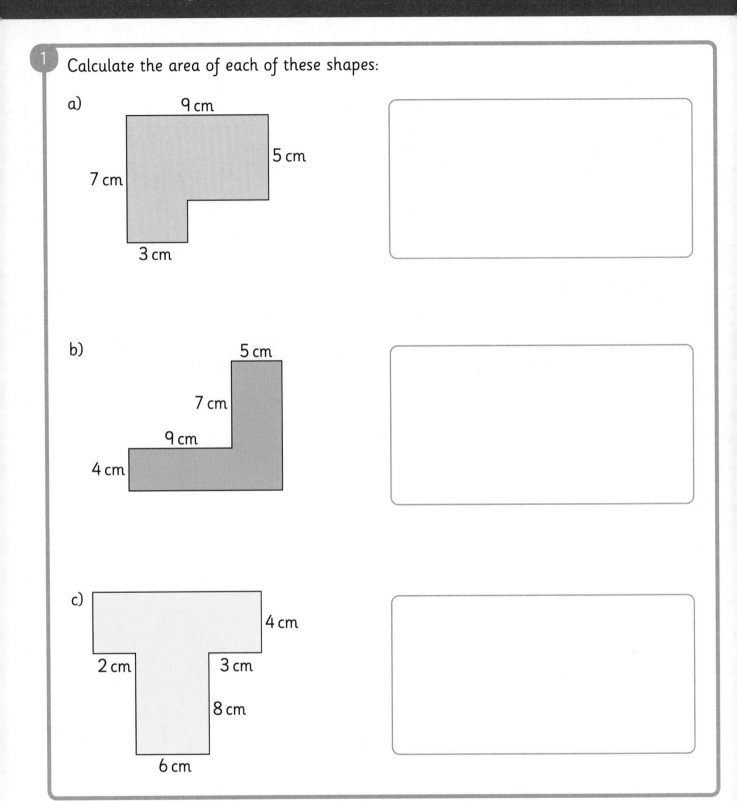

b)

c)

2 Calculate the area of each part of the community garden:

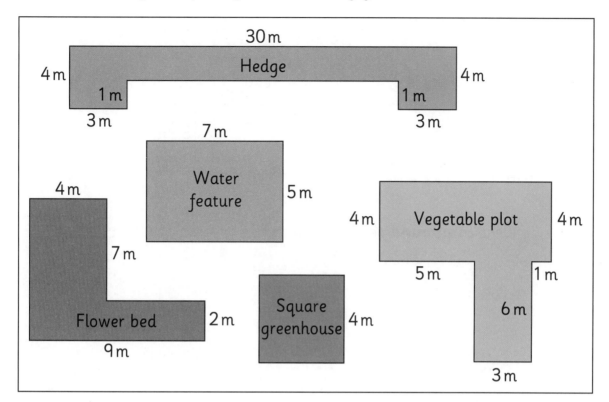

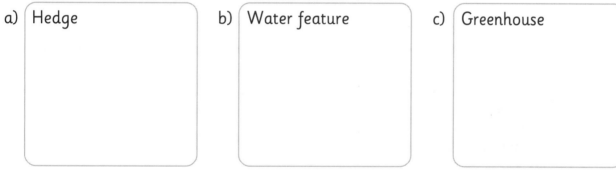

a) Hedge

b) Water feature

c) Greenhouse

d) Flower bed

e) Vegetable plot

3 The area of this compound shape is 42 cm².

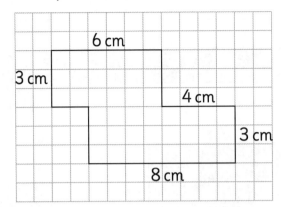

Draw a different **compound** shape that also has an area of 42 cm².

★ **Challenge**

In this compound shape, the area of A is double the area of B.

Fill in the missing lengths.

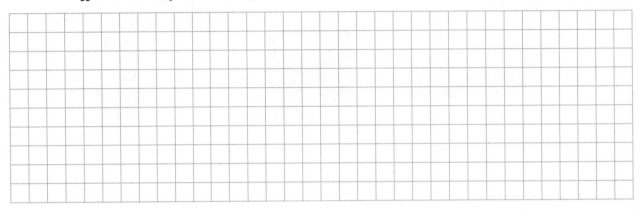

28 cm

9.10 Calculating volume

1   Calculate the volume of the following boxes. The boxes are not drawn to scale.

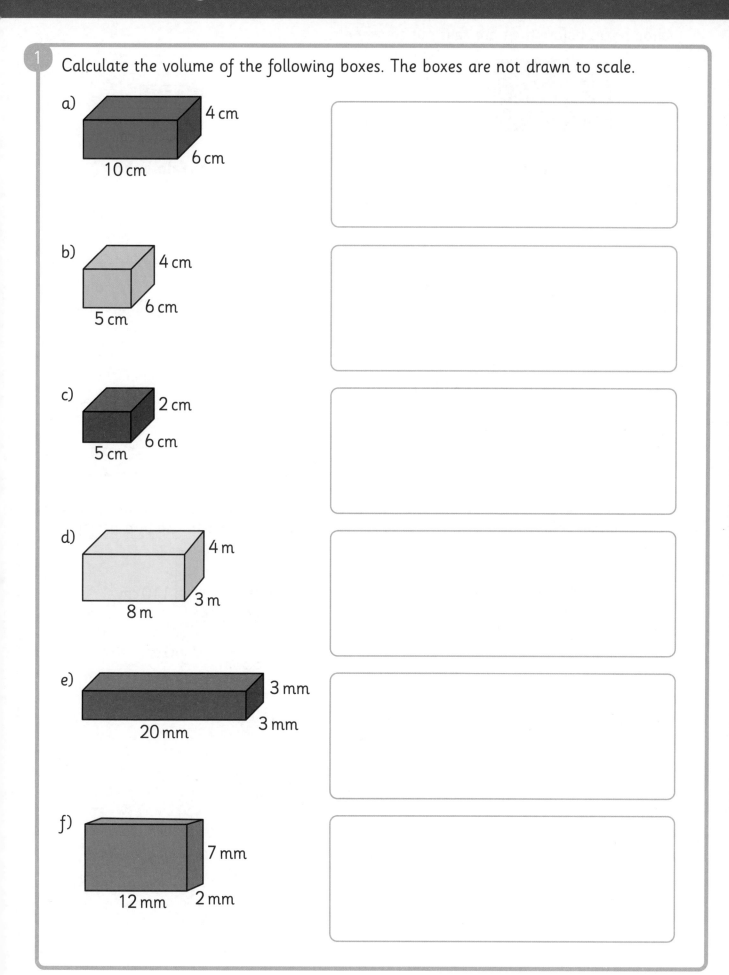

a)   4 cm   6 cm   10 cm

b)   4 cm   6 cm   5 cm

c)   2 cm   6 cm   5 cm

d)   4 m   3 m   8 m

e)   3 mm   3 mm   20 mm

f)   7 mm   12 mm   2 mm

2 A toy company is donating puzzle cubes to local schools. The cubes will be packed in shoe boxes before they are sent out to schools.

20 cm
30 cm   20 cm
shoe box

2 cm
2 cm   2 cm
puzzle cube

a) What is the volume of the puzzle cube?

b) What is the volume of the shoe box?

c) How many puzzle cubes can be packed into a shoe box?

3 The children collect these two empty boxes from a supermarket to use in a project.

POTATO CRISPS   60 cm
75 cm   50 cm

WHEAT BISCUITS   110 cm
55 cm   40 cm

Isla says: We need to use the box with the largest volume. That is the wheat biscuits box.

Nuria says: I think we should check because the potato crisps box looks larger.

Which box should the children choose? Explain your answer.

These three cuboids have equal volume. Work out what the missing lengths could be.

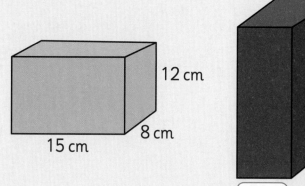

12 cm

8 cm

15 cm

48 cm

6 cm

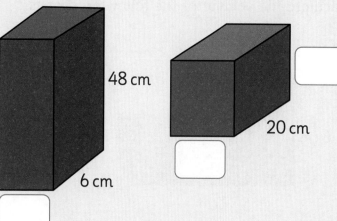

20 cm

1 Calculate the volume of the following shapes:

a)

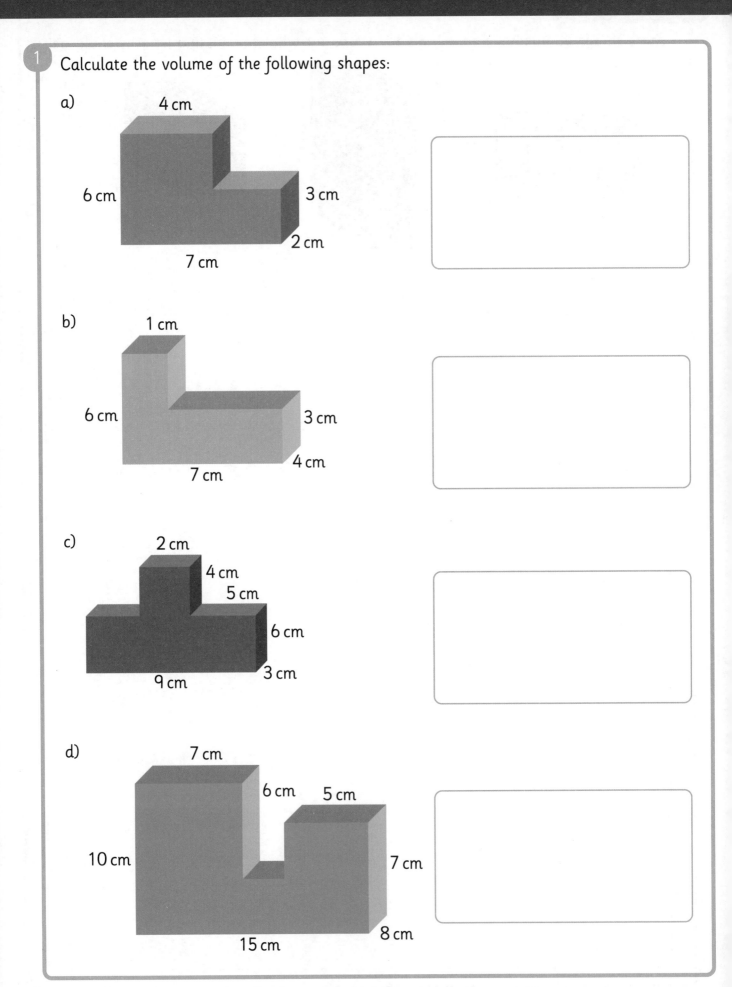

4 cm

6 cm

3 cm

2 cm

7 cm

b)

1 cm

6 cm

3 cm

4 cm

7 cm

c)

2 cm

4 cm

5 cm

6 cm

3 cm

9 cm

d)

7 cm

6 cm

5 cm

10 cm

7 cm

15 cm

8 cm

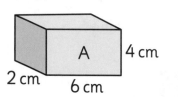 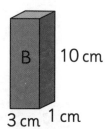 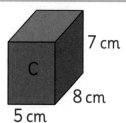 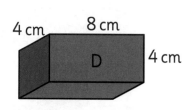

a) Which two of these cuboids can be combined to make a composite shape with a volume of 176 cm³?

b) Three of these shapes are combined to make a composite shape with a volume of 358 cm³. Which shapes are they?

3 Finlay and Nuria are working out the volume of a composite shape.

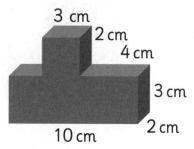

Finlay's working is shown below. Nuria says:

I partitioned it into 2 cuboids, not 3.

Show what Nuria's working could have been.

Finlay's working

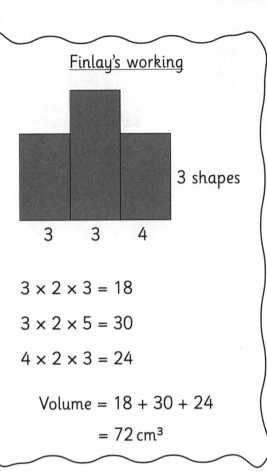

3 shapes

3   3   4

3 × 2 × 3 = 18

3 × 2 × 5 = 30

4 × 2 × 3 = 24

Volume = 18 + 30 + 24

= 72 cm³

Nuria's working

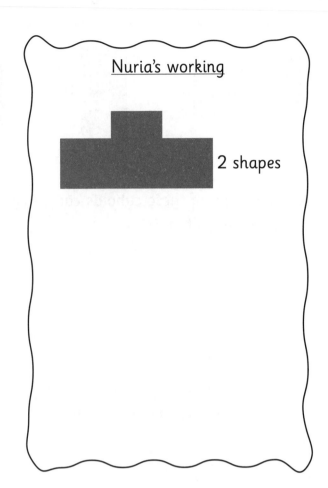

2 shapes

⭐ **Challenge**

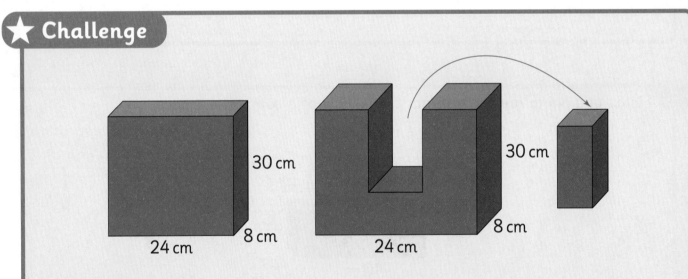

30 cm

24 cm   8 cm

30 cm

24 cm   8 cm

A piece of foam measuring 24 cm by 8 cm by 30 cm has a cuboid cut out of it so that it can be used for packing a game in a box. The volume of foam used for packing the game is 5120 cm³. What might the dimensions of the cuboid that was cut out be?

1 Calculate the capacity of each of the following containers:

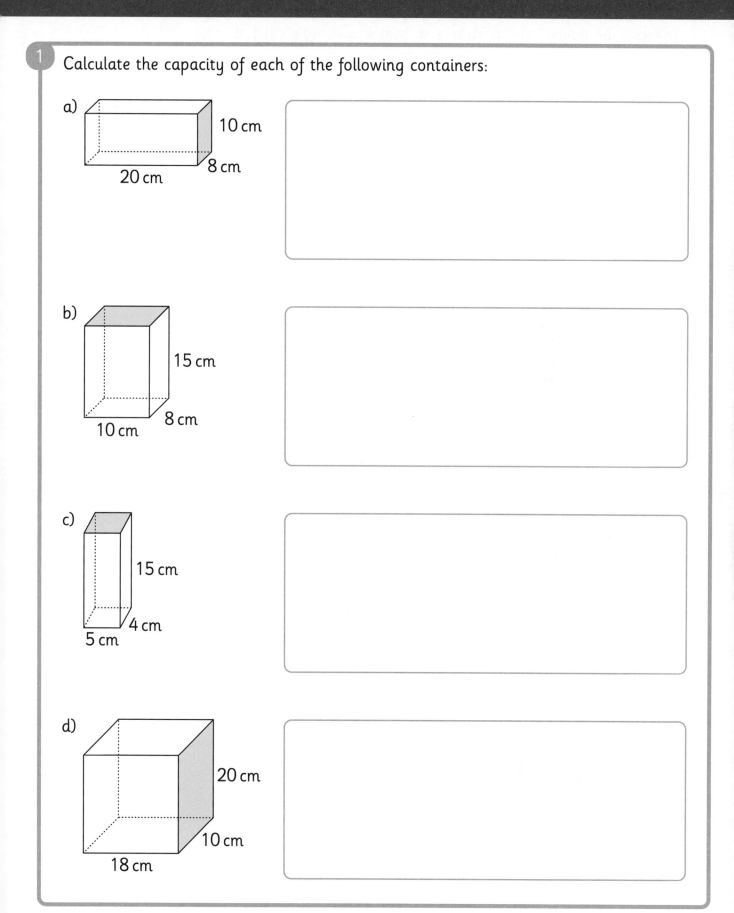

a)

10 cm

8 cm

20 cm

b)

15 cm

8 cm

10 cm

c)

15 cm

4 cm

5 cm

d)

20 cm

10 cm

18 cm

2 Each of these tanks has been partly filled with water. Work out how much water will need to be poured into each one so that it is completely full.

a)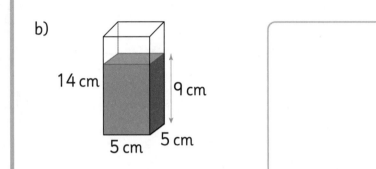
10 cm
4 cm
8 cm
12 cm

b)
14 cm
9 cm
5 cm   5 cm

c)
8 cm
2 cm
22 cm   6 cm

d)
15 cm
14 cm
15 cm
15 cm

3 Which of these tanks has the greatest capacity? Explain your answer.

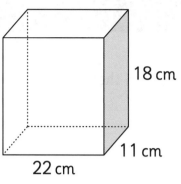

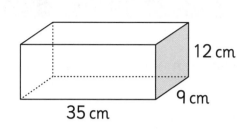

★ **Challenge**

A large fish tank in an aquarium is shown here.

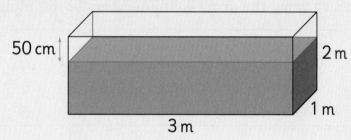

a) The water in the tank is filled to 50 cm below the top of the tank. What is the capacity of water in the tank in litres?

b) The number of goldfish in a tank is recommended as 1 per 75 litres. How many goldfish is it safe to put into this tank?

The ancient Maya civilisation only used three different symbols in their number system:

⬭   represents zero and is just a placeholder

•   represents units (or ones)

————   represents a group of five units (or ones)

For example:

• • •   represents 3 in the Maya number system because it is three ones.

• • •   represents 8 in the Maya number system because it is a group of five
————   ones and another three ones.

•   represents 11 in the Maya number system because it is two groups of
════   five ones and another one.

1   Complete this table to show the first twenty numbers in the Maya number system:

⬭	•		• • •
0	1	2	3
	————		
4	5	6	7
• • • ————			• ════
8	9	10	11
12	13	14	15
			• • • • ═══
16	17	18	19

2 The children investigate how numbers bigger than 19 were written in the Maya number system. They discover that groups of 20 were used and this was shown using two rows, one above the other.

| Number of 20s |
| Number of 1s and 5s |

represents 20   represents 26   represents 30

Write these numbers using the Maya number system.

| 20 | 23 | 25 | 27 |

| 28 | 30 | 32 | 34 |

★ Challenge

19 is the largest number that can be made using one row:

Isla and Amman are making numbers using two rows:

Isla

I have got 119. Five twenties on the top row and nineteen ones on the bottom row.

Mine is larger. It is 199. I have nine twenties on the top row and nineteen ones on the bottom row.

Amman

What do you think the largest number is that can be made using two rows?

1 These numbers have fallen out of their envelopes and are mixed up. Each envelope should have exactly four numbers that are part of a sequence of multiples in it.

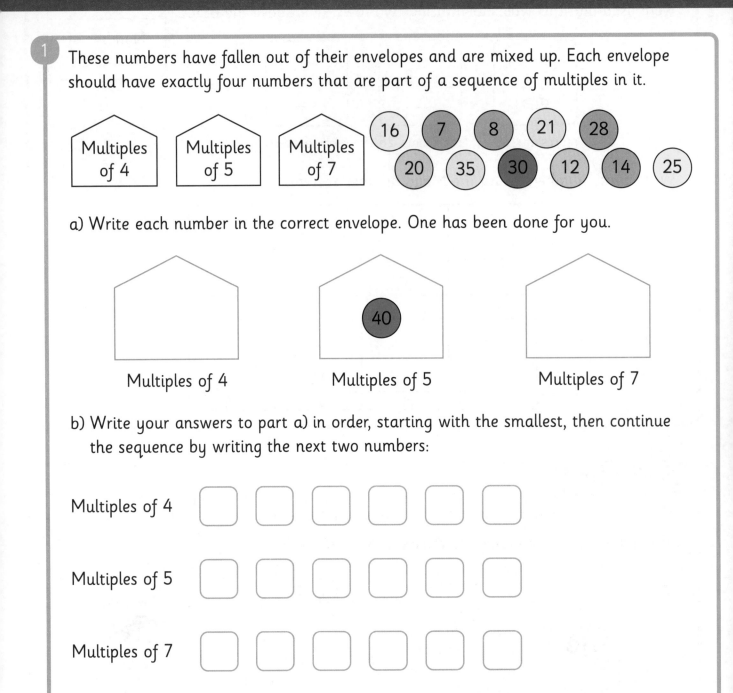

Multiples of 4   Multiples of 5   Multiples of 7

16   7   8   21   28   20   35   30   12   14   25

a) Write each number in the correct envelope. One has been done for you.

40

Multiples of 4   Multiples of 5   Multiples of 7

b) Write your answers to part a) in order, starting with the smallest, then continue the sequence by writing the next two numbers:

Multiples of 4   ☐ ☐ ☐ ☐ ☐ ☐

Multiples of 5   ☐ ☐ ☐ ☐ ☐ ☐

Multiples of 7   ☐ ☐ ☐ ☐ ☐ ☐

2 The children are showing the triangular numbers using blocks:

  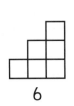 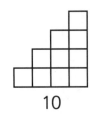

1   3   6   10

a) Draw the next triangular number using blocks.

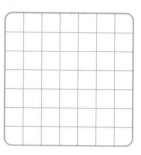

b) Amman counts the blocks that are left over.

He says:

We have 20 blocks left.

Do they have enough blocks to show the next triangular number? Explain your answer.

★ Challenge

The children read this:

Every square number can be written as the sum of two triangular numbers.

They decide to try this out for some square numbers. Can you help Nuria and Amman with their working?

Finlay
25 = 15 + 10

Isla
9 = 3 + 6

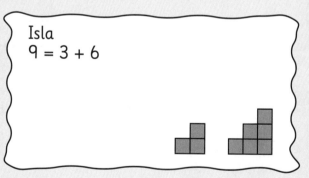

Nuria
36

Amman
81

12.1 Solving equations with inequalities

1 These scales balance because the numbers on each side have the same total. This means we can work out what the **?** stands for.

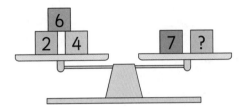

6 + 2 + 4 = 12 so, **?** is 5

Work out what the **?** stands for in these balances:

a)

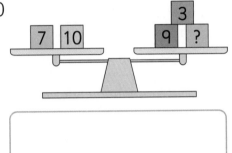

b)

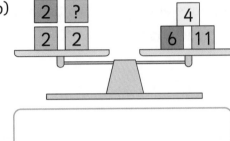

c)

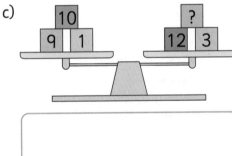

d)

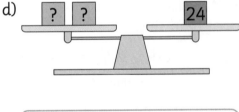

2 For these questions, find the missing numbers:

a)

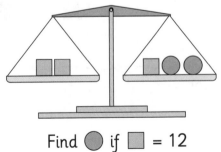

Find ⬤ if ⬛ = 12

b)

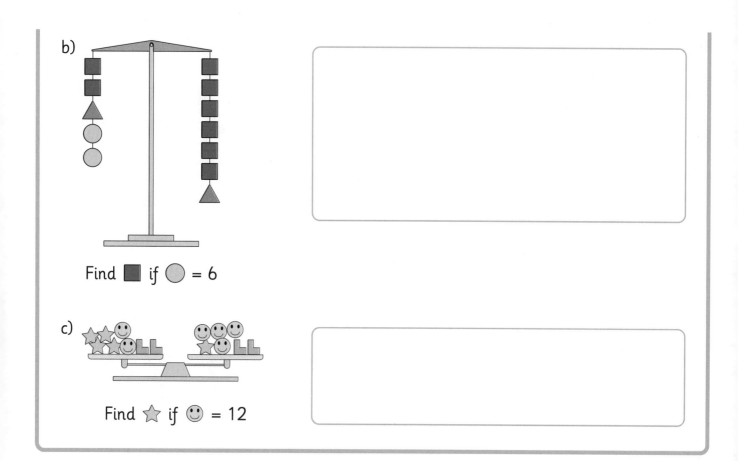

Find ■ if ○ = 6

c)

Find ☆ if ☺ = 12

3

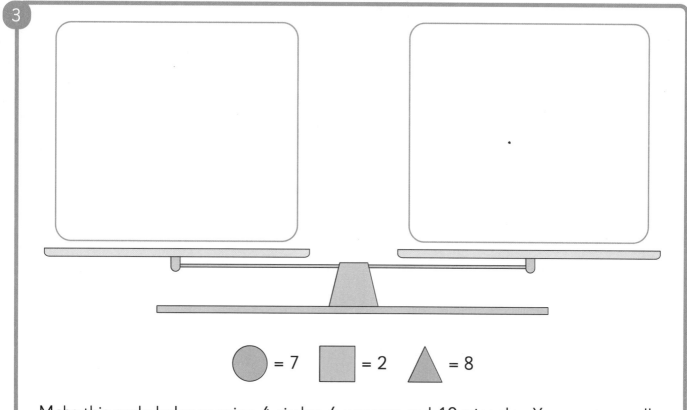

○ = 7   ■ = 2   △ = 8

Make this scale balance using 4 circles, 6 squares and 10 triangles. You must use all the shapes. Draw your solution in the answer boxes on the scales.

The two scales shown here are perfectly balanced.

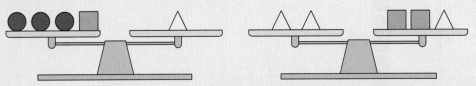

If the same shapes are used, how many circles will be needed on the right to balance these scales?

1 Add the letter that is written in each triangle into the correct column in the table.

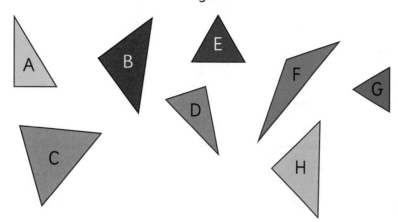

Scalene	Isosceles	Equilateral

2 Use a ruler and a protractor to help you to work out what kind of triangle each of these is.

a)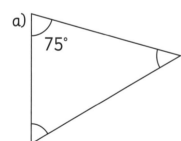

75°

b)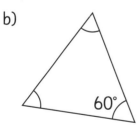

60°

c)

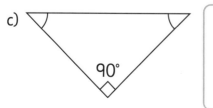

90°

d)

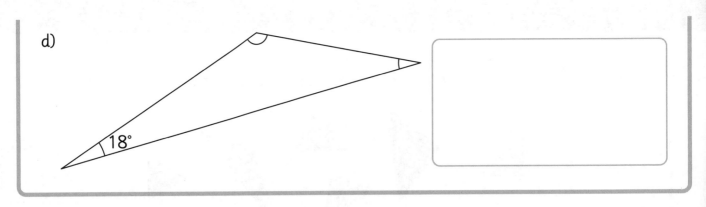

18°

---

3 Use a ruler and protractor to draw the following triangles:

a) A scalene triangle with one 50° angle.

b) An isosceles triangle with a base that is 4 cm long.

c) A scalene triangle with one side of 5 cm and one 110° angle.

d) An equilateral triangle with sides that are longer than 3 cm.

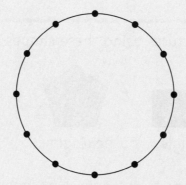

a) Join 3 points on this circle to make an isosceles triangle.

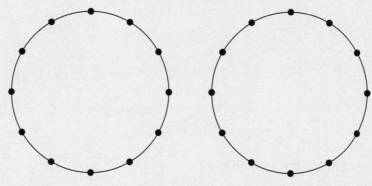

b) Find another two ways to make an isosceles triangle by joining 3 points on the circle.

Do you notice anything?

c) Join 3 points on each circle to make:

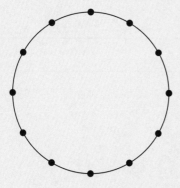

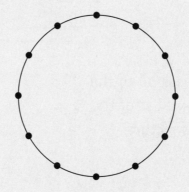

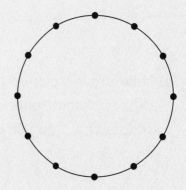

an equilateral triangle   a scalene triangle   a right-angled triangle.

1 The children are drawing pictures using these shapes:

triangles   rectangles   pentagons   hexagons   octagons

This is Amman's picture. It has a rectangle, a hexagon and 5 congruent triangles in it.

a) Draw a picture using some of these shapes. Make a list of the shapes you use in your picture.

b) Now draw a picture that uses all of the shapes at least once. Make a list of the shapes that you use in this picture.

2

a) Sketch a shape that has five straight sides of different lengths and five vertices.
Write the name of the shape beside it.

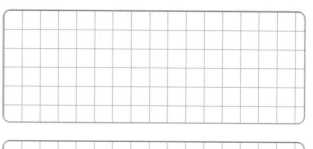

b) Sketch a shape that has four straight sides of equal length and four vertices that are **not** right angles.
Write the name of the shape beside it.

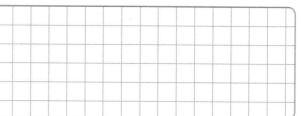

3

a) Draw three more lines to make a square.

b) Draw two more lines to make a scalene triangle.

c) Draw two more lines to make a rectangle.

★ **Challenge**

To help you in this challenge, you may use sticks or straws to make these patterns.

a) This stick pattern has six squares, five small and one large. Without moving any of the other sticks, can you take away three sticks to leave only three squares? Put a cross on each stick on the diagram that needs to be removed.

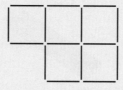

b) This pattern has eight small equilateral triangles. It is made from sixteen sticks. Without moving any of the other sticks, can you take away four sticks to leave four small equilateral triangles? Put a cross on each stick on the diagram that needs to be removed.

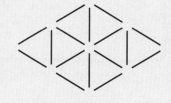

1 Complete each of these partially completed drawings of prisms.

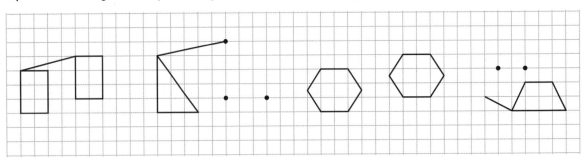

2 a) How many straws and how many blobs of modelling clay are needed to make the skeleton of this cube?

b) Draw a line to match each 3D object to the pile of straws and clay blobs needed to build it. The straws can be cut if required.

3D object	Square based pyramid	Triangular prism	Cuboid	Hexagonal prism
Pile of straws and clay blobs	9 straws 6 blobs	12 straws 8 blobs	8 straws 5 blobs	18 straws 12 blobs

3 Name each of the 3D objects being described here. Make a sketch of each one.

a) This 3D object has six square faces and eight vertices.

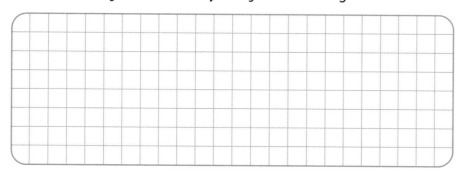

Name

b) This 3D object has three rectangular faces, two triangular faces and six vertices.

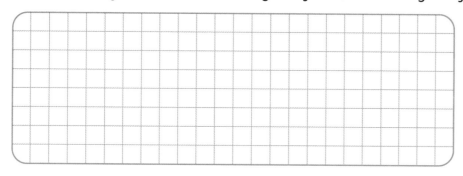

Name

c) This 3D object has four triangular faces, one square face and five vertices.

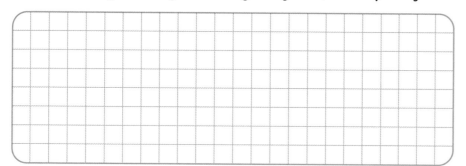

Name

★ **Challenge**

An architect uses exactly 1·5 m of wire to make this triangular prism as part of a model.

How long is the prism?

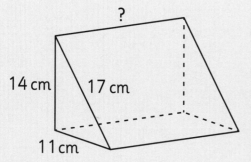

14 cm   17 cm

11 cm

1 Name the 3D objects from their nets:

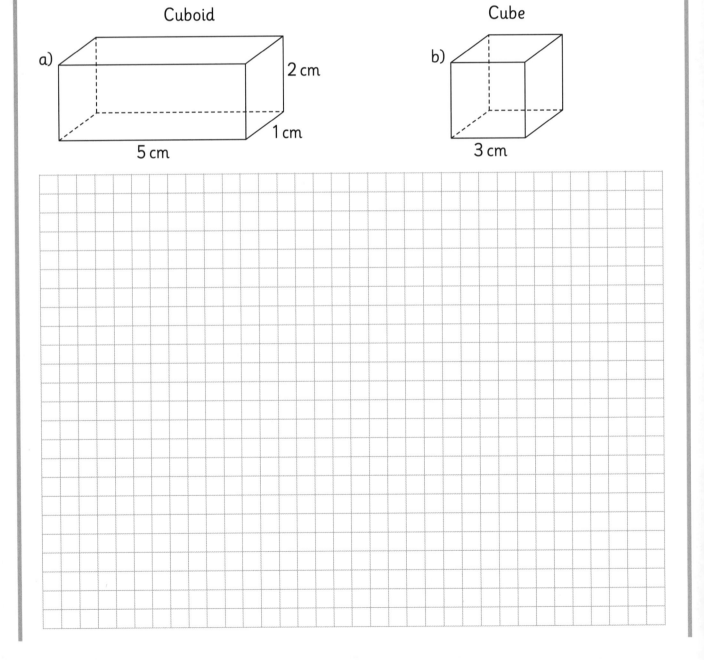

a)

b)

c)

d)

2 Draw an accurate net for each of these 3D objects.

Cuboid

Cube

a)

2 cm

1 cm

5 cm

b)

3 cm

Triangular prism

c)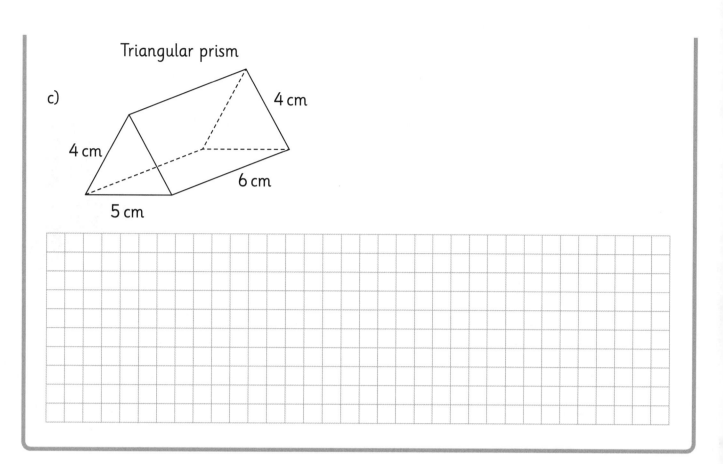

4 cm

4 cm

6 cm

5 cm

3 This cuboid is drawn on isometric paper. Draw its net on the grid.

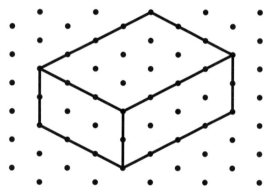

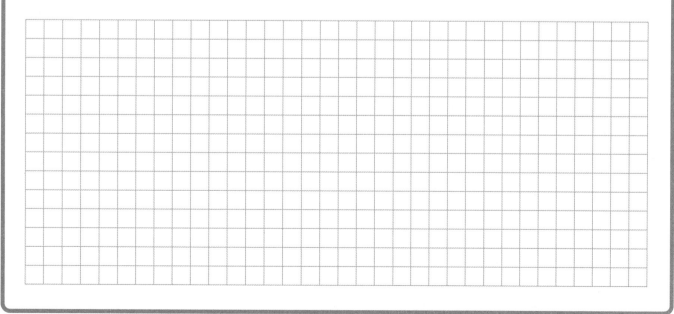

As part of a design challenge the children are making a model of a tower block.

They make nets of a cuboid with a triangular prism on one end.

Amman and Isla

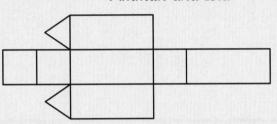

Finlay and Nuria

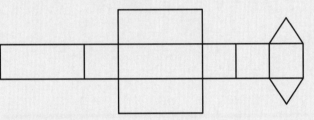

a) When they cut out the nets and try to build the 3D object, only one of them works. Which one works? Explain what happens with the other one?

b) Draw your own net for this object.

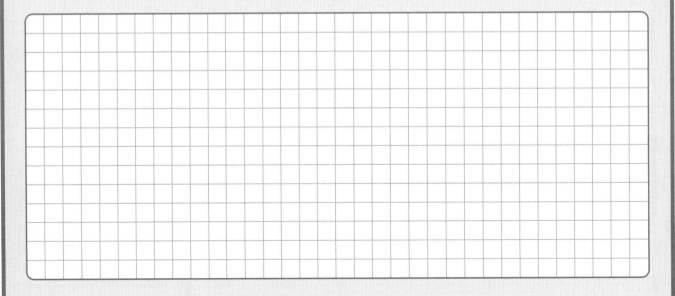

1 Draw these triangles accurately using a ruler and a protractor then measure the missing angle in each one. (The diagrams are not drawn to scale.)

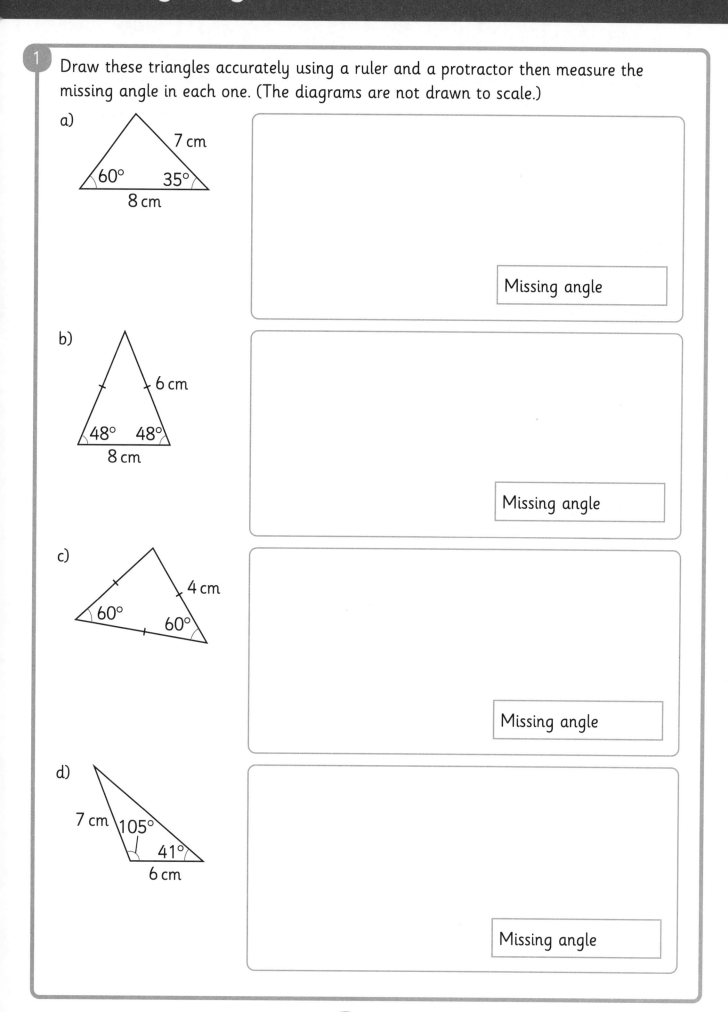

a)

7 cm
60°   35°
8 cm

Missing angle

b)

6 cm
48°   48°
8 cm

Missing angle

c)

4 cm
60°   60°

Missing angle

d)

7 cm 105°
41°
6 cm

Missing angle

2 The children are following these instructions to make an accurate drawing of an isosceles triangle:

Step 1: Draw a horizontal line 6 cm long close to the bottom of the answer box.

Step 2: Write letter A at the left-hand end of this line and letter B at the right-hand end of this line.

Step 3: Measure an angle of 46° from point A for the interior angle of the triangle.

Step 4: Draw a line 4·3 cm long from point A to make the interior angle of 46°.

Step 5: Measure an angle of 46° from point B to make another interior angle of the triangle.

Step 6: Draw a line 4·3 cm long from point B to make the interior angle of 46°.

Nuria and Isla both went wrong. Here are their attempts:

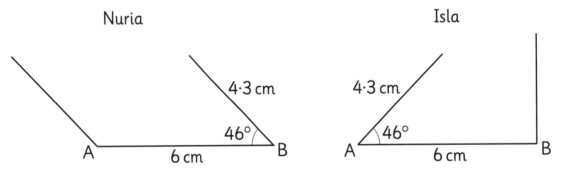

Nuria

Isla

a) Follow the steps in the instructions to draw the triangle correctly using a ruler and a protractor.

b) Use a protractor to measure the size
   of the third angle in your triangle.

c) Describe what Nuria and Isla did wrong.

⭐ **Challenge**

Accurately draw each of these triangles in the box below (continue on a separate piece of paper if you need to):

a) two different isosceles triangles with an angle of 40°

b) a scalene triangle with sides measuring 5 cm, 5·5 cm and 6 cm

c) a right-angled triangle with sides measuring 15 mm, 36 mm and 39 mm

d) an equilateral triangle with sides measuring 4 cm.

1 Find the reflex angles that are **inside** this shape. Mark them with an arc on the diagram.

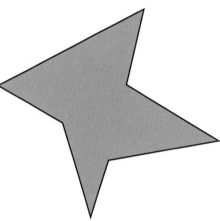

2

a) Measure the acute angle and the reflex angle here.

b) Measure the obtuse angle and the reflex angle here.

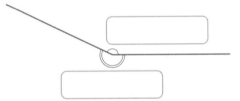

Measure these reflex angles.

c)

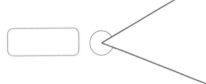

d)

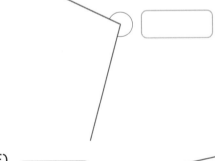

e)

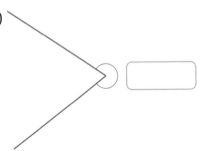

f)

3 Draw the following reflex angles.

a) 250°

b) 305°

a) Draw an example of a quadrilateral (a four-sided shape) that has a reflex angle as one of its **interior** angles.

b) Draw an example of a pentagon (a five-sided shape) with reflex angles for two of its **interior** angles.

c) Draw a shape with several **interior reflex** angles. Can you find out and write the name of your shape?

1 Calculate the missing angles:

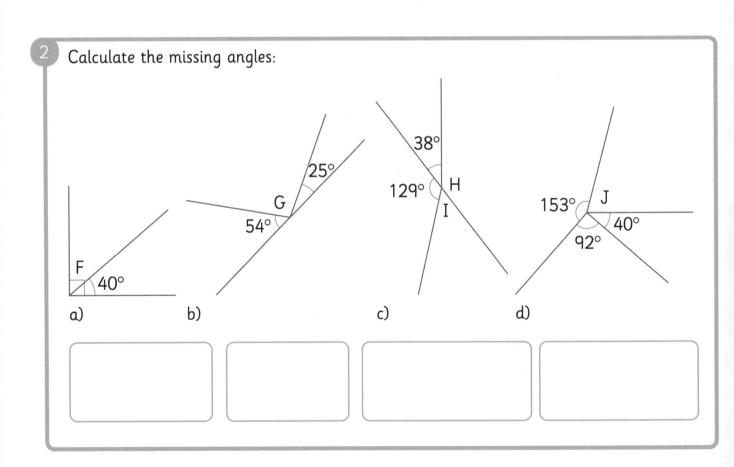

a)

b)

c)

d)

2 Calculate the missing angles:

a)

b)

c)

d)

3 The children have some angle cards.

A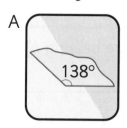

B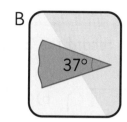

C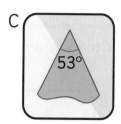

D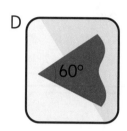

E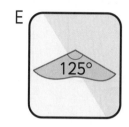

F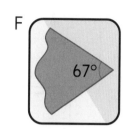

a) Which two cards fit together exactly to make a right angle?

b) Which three cards fit together exactly on a straight line?

c) Which four cards fit together exactly around a point?

⭐ **Challenge**

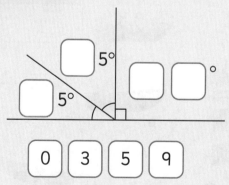

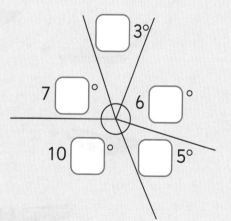

Use the digit cards to fill in the missing numbers in each of these. You can only use each digit card once.

99

1 Use a protractor to measure then record the 3-figure bearing of point B from point A in each of these.

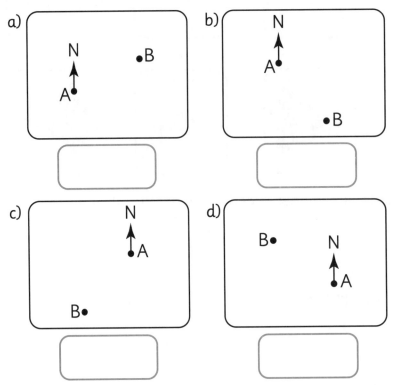

a)

b)

c)

d)

2 Use a protractor to measure then record the 3-figure bearing of each boat from the lighthouse.

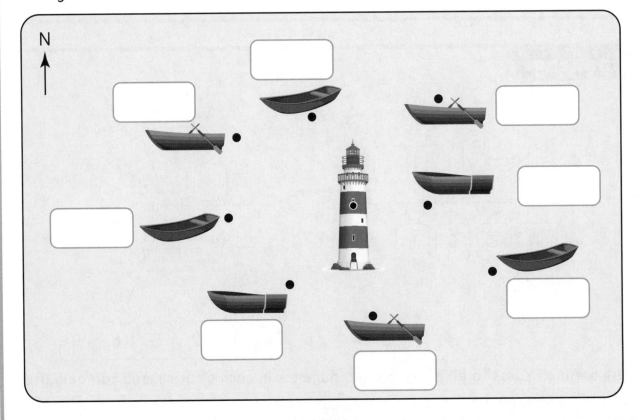

This shows an air traffic control radar screen at an airport. The distance between each circle represents 10 km.

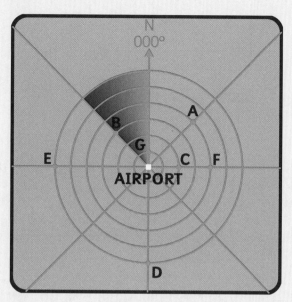

a) Aeroplane A is 40 km from the airport on a bearing of 045°. How far is aeroplane B from the airport and what is its 3-figure bearing?

b) Aeroplane A and aeroplane F are both 40 km from the airport. Identify another pair of aeroplanes that are the same distance away from the airport and give the 3-figure bearing for each one.

c) The aeroplane that is closest to the airport is preparing to land. Which aeroplane is this and what is its bearing?

d) Aeroplane H is 50 km away from the airport and is approaching from the Southwest. Mark aeroplane H on the diagram and write down its 3-figure bearing.

1. This map shows a holiday island with some of the attractions marked.

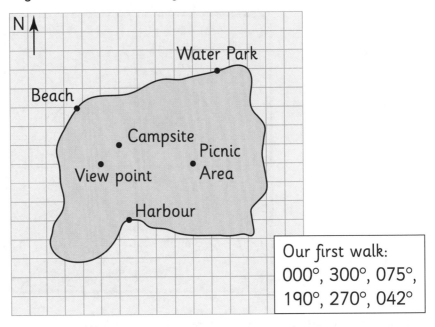

Our first walk:
000°, 300°, 075°,
190°, 270°, 042°

Finlay and his family arrive at the **harbour** by boat. Finlay keeps a note of the 3-figure bearings of their first walk around the island so that he can draw the walk on the map.

Show the family's walk on the map and list the attractions they visited in order.

Harbour

2. The children have written a code for a small programmable turtle toy to move around on a page.

Follow these instructions and plot the journey using a ruler and protractor.

3 cm on a bearing of 115°, then 7 cm on a bearing of 265°, then 6 cm on a bearing of 025°, then 4 cm on a bearing of 094°, then 5 cm on a bearing of 126°, then 5·5 cm on a bearing of 260°.

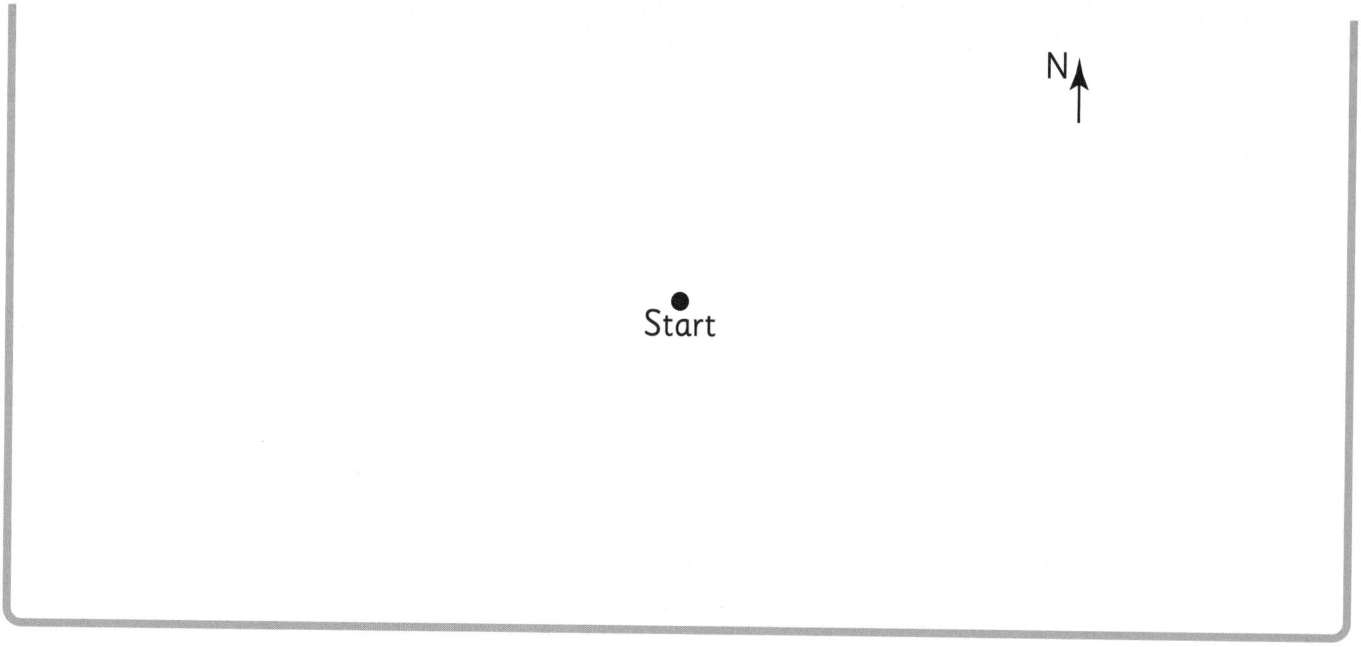

N ↑

Start

Checkpoint 1

N ↑

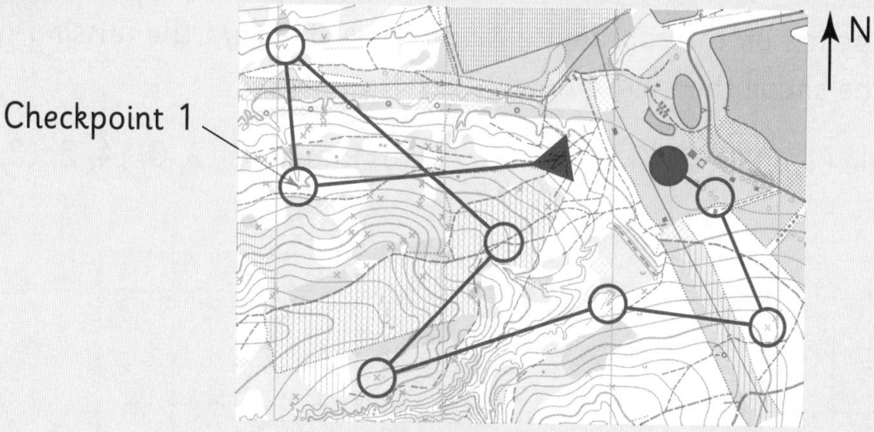

This is a map of an orienteering course. It begins at the ◄ and ends at the ●. If 1 cm on the map represents 1 km on the ground, complete the table then describe the journey around the course using three figure bearings and distances in km.

Section of the course	Distance	3-figure bearing
Start to checkpoint 1		

14.6 Using coordinates

1 Calculate the missing coordinates for each shape.

a)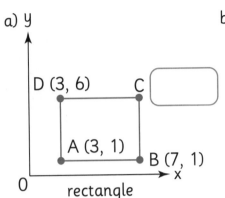

rectangle

b)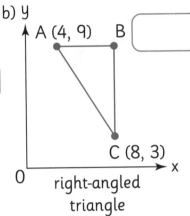

right-angled
triangle

c)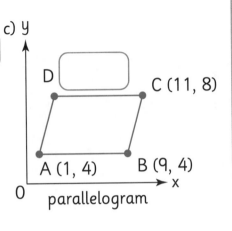

parallelogram

2 Plot these points on the coordinate diagram given. Mark the missing point to complete the shape then write down its coordinates.

a) Rectangle (1, 2) (5, 2) (5, 5)

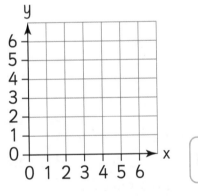

(,   )

b) Rhombus (2, 0) (4, 3) (2, 6)

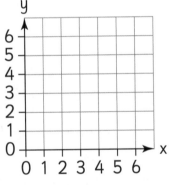

(,   )

c) Square (1, 3) (4, 1) (6, 4)

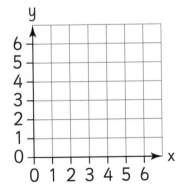

(,   )

d) Isosceles triangle (3, 0) (6, 5)

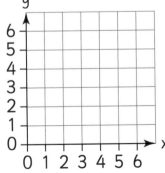

(,   )

3

a) The coordinates for two vertices of a kite are shown here. What could the coordinates of the other vertices be?

> [ ]

Can you find another solution?

> [ ]

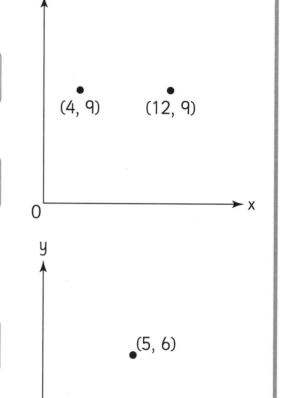

b) The coordinates for two vertices of a square are shown here. What could the coordinates of the other vertices be?

> [ ]

Can you find another solution?

> [ ]

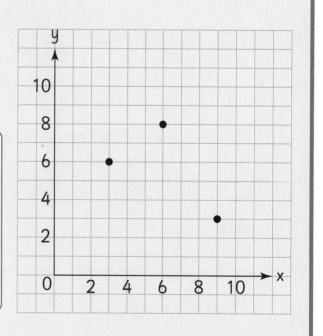

★ **Challenge**

Three vertices of a hexagon are shown here. Add another three vertices to the diagram to complete a hexagon. Write down the coordinates of each vertex.

> [ ]

14.7 Symmetry 1

1 Draw all the lines of symmetry onto these shapes.

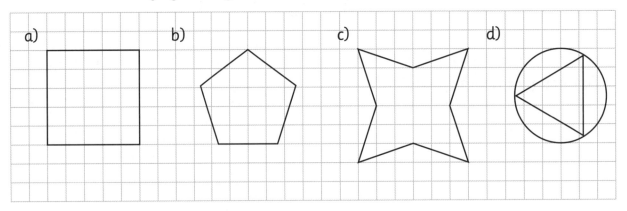

a)   b)   c)   d)

2 a) Work out how many lines of symmetry each of these shapes has and draw them in.

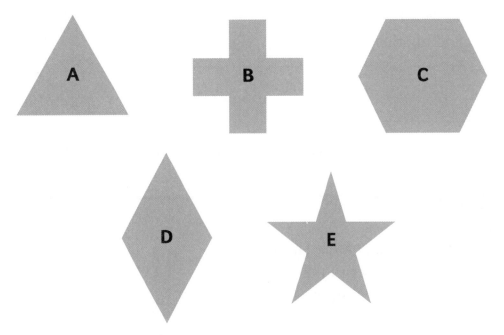

A   B   C

D   E

b) Complete the table by listing the shapes in order, starting with the one that has the fewest lines of symmetry.

Shape					
Number of lines of symmetry					

3 This diagram shows a square drawn inside a regular octagon.

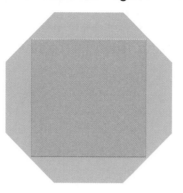

a) Draw all the lines of symmetry on the shape.

b) How do you know that you have found **all** the lines of symmetry?

★ **Challenge**

The children are researching flags. They find out that the flag of Switzerland is a square flag that has four lines of symmetry.

Design a flag with exactly four lines of symmetry. Use at least two different colours in your flag design.

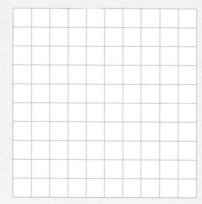

14.8 Symmetry 2

1 Complete the shapes by reflecting them in the lines of symmetry. Make sure the colours are symmetrical too.

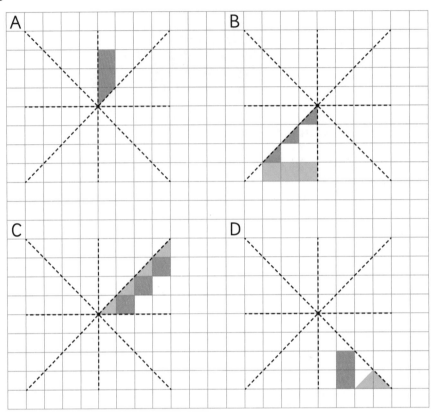

2 Complete this design to give it four lines of symmetry.

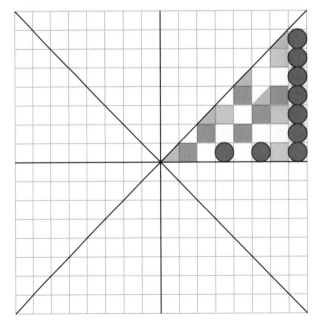

3 Nuria says:

> This pattern should have four lines of symmetry, but it doesn't look right.

Amman says:

> You are correct. I can see some errors.

a) How many can you see in the diagram?

> There are _____ errors.

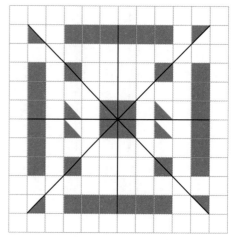

b) Add some shading to the diagram so that it has exactly four lines of symmetry.

★ **Challenge**

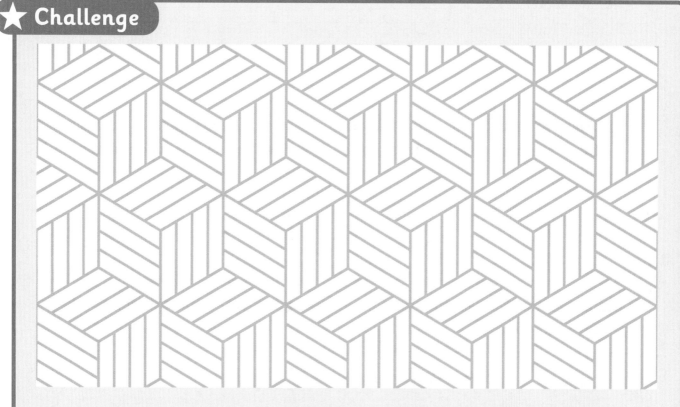

Use coloured shading to create a symmetrical pattern on this hexagonal design. How many lines of symmetry can you include in your pattern?

1 This map of a country park is drawn using a scale of 1 cm : 500 m.

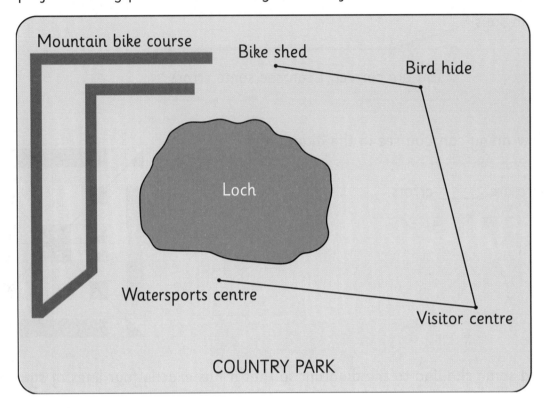

a) What is the actual distance between the visitor centre and the water sports centre?

b) The children visit the country park with their bikes. They cycle from the visitor centre to the bird hide then to the bike shed. How far did they cycle altogether?

c) Isla and Amman decide to go around the mountain bike course. Work out the length of the course.

2 The children are drawing a map for a school fete. They measure the distances with a trundle wheel and the directions with a compass.

The face painting is 150 m north of the park entrance, the refreshment stall is 200 m north-west of the park entrance, the archery is 125 m south-east of the refreshment stall and the balloon modelling is 175 m south-west of the face painting.

N ↑

X
Park entrance

a) Using a scale of 1 cm : 25 m, and a protractor, mark where the face painting, refreshment stall, archery and balloon modelling areas are accurately on the map.

b) A first aid ✚ area needs to be positioned at least 75 m away from the park entrance and no more than 50 m away from the archery. Add the ✚ symbol to a suitable place for the first aid area on the map.

★ **Challenge**

The children find an old road atlas in a school cupboard.

They measure the width of each page to be 18 cm and work out from the maps that this represents 63 km.

Find the scale of the maps in the atlas.

GREAT BRITAIN

Easy to read Large scale

1 Write a word or phrase from this list to complete each of these sentences.

| sample | | population | | big question | | data |

a) _____ is a word we use to describe information.

b) In data handling, a _____ is the entire group information is being gathered from.

c) A _____ only gathers data from some of the people who can take part.

d) A _____ highlights what the researcher wants to find out about.

2 Decide whether each of these surveys gathers data from a whole population or from a sample. Explain your thinking for each one. The first one has been done for you.

a) A drama group for children aged between 8 and 15 years old asks everyone in the group who is aged 8, 9 and 10 what their favourite musical film is.

Whole population / ⟨Sample⟩	This is a sample because it only involves some of the children. It misses out the older ones.

b) All of the players in a rugby union team are asked to look at three team strip designs and choose their favourite.

Whole population / Sample	

c) Everyone who visits a leisure centre on a Monday afternoon is asked if they would like the café to sell fresh fruit.

Whole population / Sample	

3 Complete this table to show how data could be gathered from a whole population or from a sample to answer a big question. The first one has been done for you.

Big question	Whole population	Sample
What reading genre do the members of a book club prefer?	All the members of the book club	Every fifth name on an alphabetical list of book club members
How do pupils in a school travel to school each day?		
Which game do members of a virtual gaming club like best?		
Which breed of dog is most popular in a dog agility club?		

★ Challenge

A cinema manager wants to find out what genre of film is most popular with adults living in the local area. They decide to ask their staff to speak to people as they leave the cinema, having watched a popular family-friendly animated movie in the school holidays.

a) Do you think the cinema manager will gather useful data here? Explain your thinking.

b) Suggest two alternative ways that the cinema manager might gather data.

1.

2.

1 Say whether each of these graphs is accurate or misleading and explain why.

a) Number of tickets sold

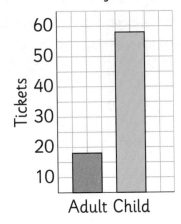

Accurate or misleading?

b) Rainfall over 5 days

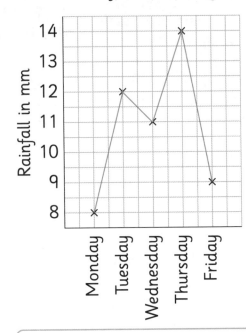

Accurate or misleading?

c) Favourite dance style

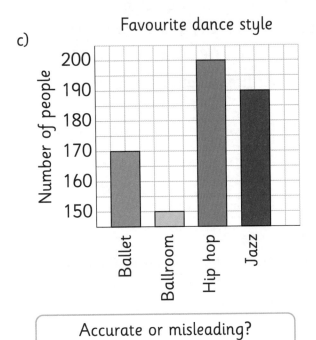

Accurate or misleading?

d) Money raised this year

Accurate or misleading?

An advertising company is designing an advert for a new type of compost. A designer presents two different possibilities, each including a graph based on data provided about the average height of sunflowers planted in the compost.

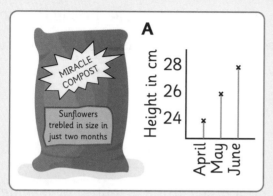

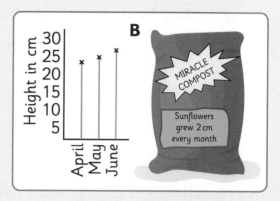

a) Which advert do you think might encourage more people to buy the compost? Explain your answer.

b) Which advert is more trustworthy? Explain your answer.

15.3 Understanding sampling bias

1 For each of these big questions, say whether the sample is biased or unbiased. Explain your answer for each one.

a) **Big question:** What activities do young people enjoy doing in the summer holiday?

Sample: young people taking part in a musical theatre summer school experience.

b) **Big question:** Do young people in a school prefer using a laptop or a tablet when doing research in class?

Sample: every fifth name on the register for each class.

2 The children looked at each of these and decided that the samples are not good representations of the whole population. Why do you think they decided this? Explain your thinking.

	Big question	Sample	Explanation
a)	Which funfair ride is most popular?	People queuing for a rollercoaster ride at the funfair.	
b)	Which day are people most likely to go to a supermarket?	Shoppers in a supermarket at the weekend.	
c)	Which author is most popular with people aged 12 or under?	Adult customers in a bookshop.	

3 Suggest a sample that would be a good representation of the whole population for each of the big questions in question 2.

	Big question	Unbiased sample
a)	Which funfair ride is most popular?	
b)	Which day are people most likely to go to a supermarket?	
c)	Which author is most popular with people aged 12 or under?	

★ **Challenge**

The children read a newspaper article that interests them.

School traffic issues

Over the last 20 years, the number of children being driven to school has doubled. In some areas, one in every five cars on the road at 8·50 am is going to school.

They decide to inquire into how many children in their school are driven there regularly by car.

a) What might the children's big question be?

b) How might the children collect data in a way that avoids bias?

1 There are 60 children in Primary 7. They have each been asked to choose one of these items of clothing as a leavers gift from the parent council: hoodie, polo shirt, rugby top, waterproof jacket.

Their choices are displayed in this pie chart.

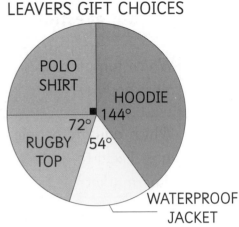

LEAVERS GIFT CHOICES

a) What was the least popular choice?

b) What percentage of the children chose a polo shirt?

c) How many children chose a hoodie?

★ Challenge

Riverside School and Parkway School took part in a sports festival. These pie charts show some information about the medals each school won.

RIVERSIDE SCHOOL

PARKWAY SCHOOL

a) If Riverside school won seven bronze medals, how many gold medals did they win?

b) A teacher says, "The pie charts show that Riverside School won more gold medals than Parkway School." Is this correct? Explain your thinking.

16.1 Predicting and explaining the outcomes of simple chance situations and experiments

1 The children have a set of 12 cards with numbers on them:

5   9   5   8   5   9   9   9   5   9   5   5

a) Amman chooses a card at random. What is the probability that it has a 5 on it?

b) Isla chooses a card at random from the set of 12 cards. What is the probability of Isla choosing an odd number?

2 A bag contains 8 red counters, 6 blue counters and 10 yellow counters.

a) What is the probability of choosing a blue counter from the bag?

b) What is the probability of **not** choosing a yellow counter from the bag?

c) 12 purple counters are added to the bag. What is the probability of picking a purple counter from the bag?

Challenge

The children are playing a game by throwing a ball at
this target. They start with 24 points and aim to get
to zero by taking away their score with each throw.
The shaded parts in the centre are worth double score,
so this throw is worth 14.

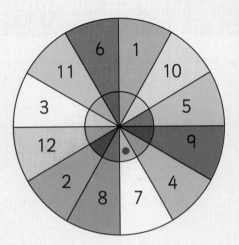

a) These diagrams show Amman and Finlay's first throws.

Amman

Finlay

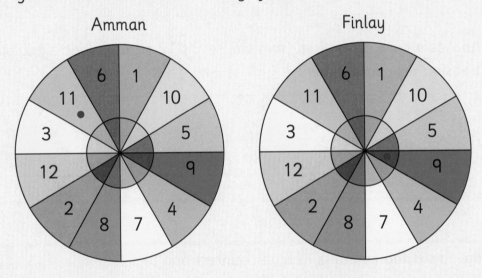

Amman says: Oh no, I can't win with my next throw.

Finlay says: I need to score 6. I can win with my
next throw in two different ways.

What are the two different ways for Finlay to score 6?

b) Which numbers have the highest probability of being scored with one throw?
   What is this probability?